GH00584797

Famous Pugilists
of the
English Prize Ring
1719–1870

Mick Hill

An environmentally friendly book printed and bound in England by
www.printondemand-worldwide.com

Mixed Sources
Product group from well-managed
forests, and other controlled sources

FSC
This book is made from materials

PEFC Certified
This product is
from sustainably
managed forests
and controlled

201209025

www.fast-print.net/store.php

Famous Pugilists of the English Prize Ring 1719 - 1870
Copyright © Mick Hill 2013

All rights reserved

No part of this book may be reproduced in any form by photocopying
or any electronic or mechanical means, including information storage
or retrieval systems, without permission in writing from both the
copyright owner and the publisher of the book.

ISBN 978-178035-505-4

WEST SUSSEX LIBRARY SERVICE	
20 1209025	
UPF	4/13
796.83	

First published 2013 by
FASTPRINT PUBLISHING
Peterborough, England.

Contents
Champions of England

Middleweights

Lightweights

Featherweights

Bantamweights

Acknowledgements

Bare Fists – *Bob Mee*
Up to Scratch – *Tony Gee*
Champions by Acclaim – *Alan MacDonald*
Prizefighting: The Age of Regency Boximania – *John Ford*
Strange Encounters– *James Brady*
Bare Fist Fighters of the 18th & 19th Century –
  Dick Johnson
The Bareknuckle Breed – *Louis Golding*
Master of the Ring – *Graham Gordon*
Fights for the Championship – *Frank L. Downing*
Boxiana – *Pearce Egan*
Fights for the Championship and Other Battles –
  Fred W. J. Henning
Pugilistica – *Henry Downes Miles*
Famous Fights and Fighters – *Charles Platt*
John Gully and his times – *Bernard Darwin*
Fisticuffs and Personalities of the Prize Ring –
  Harry E. Cleveland
Bareknuckles – *Dennis Brailford*
Jack Scroggins – *R. A. Hartley*
The Milling Men of the Old Prize Ring – *Alan McDonald*
The Bareknuckle Record Book – *Bill Matthews*
The Bareknuckle Record Book – *Jan Skotnicki*
Reading Mercury 1789-1903
Berkshire Chronicle 1825-1912
BoxRec Boxing Records

*Thanks particularly to Bill Matthews of St Austell, Cornwall
and Tracy Callis of the Cyber Boxing Zone for their kind
permission to use their illustrations.*

Foreword

This book is an attempt to portray all the so called Champions of the English Prize Ring and many of the most prominent pugilists of the lighter weights, from the generally agreed beginning of bare knuckle prize fighting, starting with James Figg in 1719, up until its demise in England around 1870. This was due to a gradual and increasing number of fighters starting to use gloves, as recommended in the Queensbury Rules of 1867, for the fighters own safety. Those who refused to give up the old style found it increasingly difficult to obtain paid fights in England so left these shores, mostly for America where bare fist fighting was still popular.

As there was no established governing body for the sport until the late 19th century, exact weight divisions until then are somewhat obscure. In the beginning men weighing approximately 166lb. (73kg.) and upwards fought each other and generally the most successful one of all could acclaimed by the Fancy (the supporters of boxing), the sporting press, their trainers and backers and in many cases by the boxers themselves, to be the Champion of England. Lighter men had no choice but to take on heavier men most of the time, until the lighter Daniel Mendoza (only a middleweight or light heavyweight today) won the Championship of England in the 1790's, increasing the popularity of the number of smaller men entering the prize ring against each other and gaining their own weight recognition. This resulted in these lighter weights being given the general classification or term of middleweight, lightweight and a little later, featherweight and bantamweight. Even so weight limits were not set in stone compared with today, so variances and sometimes great variances still occurred; however these were generally sorted out when contracts or articles were drawn up before a fight, with weight stipulations and purse restrictions. If a fighter then failed to turn up or make the agreed weight he forfeited his stake. For the sake of this book I have classified the approximate lighter weights as Middleweight up to 161lb., or approx. 73kg., Lightweight up to 140lb., or approx. 63½kg., Featherweight up to 126lb., or approx. 57kg., and Bantamweight up to 116lb or approx. 52½kg. The top men in these lighter divisions were not called Champions of England, unlike the heaviest weight division, but mostly given the accolade by the Fancy etc., as the best in the land in their class or at that particular weight at that particular time, or the pugilists and their associates just claimed the title themselves.

Many fights over the history of the prize ring were fixed and the sport had its high and low periods with a mixture of great champions and contenders along with many scoundrels and cheats. At times this reputation dragged the sport almost into oblivion until an honest and true pugilist or pugilists saved the day by making the sport honourable again.

There are many boxers not in this book, some that boxing historians more eminent and knowledgeable than this author will call champions or leading contenders and feeling they should have been mentioned, however if I named all the pugilists that might have a legitimate claim to various titles and accolades then this book could possibly have run into hundreds of pages!

THE CHAMPIONS OF ENGLAND

James Figg
(Champion of England 1719-1730)

Born: 1695   Died: 1734

"The First Champion of England"

Commonly accepted as being the first Champion of England, James Figg was born in the Oxfordshire village of Thame, the youngest of seven children. He was from a poor family and his early life would have been hard in this small agricultural village, with very little work around apart from toiling on the land. Where he got his prowess with cudgel, quarterstaff, sword and fist fighting is not known, although he probably visited the booths at local fairs in the area, so these skills were probably learnt and honed there.

He stood about 6' 0" tall, weighed approximately 185lbs. and it was the Earl of Peterborough who apparently, as the story goes, first spotted James Figg exercising his skills on the village green in Thame and invited him to London. As Figg had made his headquarters at the Greyhound Inn in Thame, it is more likely the Earl had met him there while stopping over on his way back to the capital. This might have been around 1714, as it is reported that Figg was working under Timothy Buck of Clare Market at this time. Impressed with the pugilist's skills, the nobleman backed Figg with hard cash, allowing him to open an academy in an old building called the Adam and Eve in Tottenham Court Road, London, then a tree-lined country lane, in or around 1719. Here he passed on his martial art skills as well as fist fighting to others wanting to become pugilists and also prominent people of the day, such as writer Jonathan Swift, artist William Hogarth and the well-known Captain Barclay. This also attracted members of the nobility and royals to watch them and to learn skills themselves, thought necessary to acquire for self-protection in the dangerous streets and back alleys of Regency London. Here with his stable of other highly skilled pugilists, contests or exhibitions were held involving all the disciplines, boxing and wrestling, cudgel, broad staff and sword and you were judged the winner or loser on each skill before being judged an overall winner.

As he had beaten all opponents who dared to challenge him, Figg had declared himself as the Champion of England in 1719 at Southwark Fair and then from 1720-1723 he defeated many challengers, including Timothy Buck, Tom Stokes, Chris Clarkson and Bill Flanders to further enhance his reputation of being the best in the land. He owed his success in the ring though more through his strength and courage rather than boxing skill, severely punishing his victims with powerful blows and superior skills in the other areas of competition, especially with the broad staff.

Boxing became increasingly popular and by 1723 on the orders of George I, a ring was erected in Hyde Park for use by the general public, another ring was run by someone known only as "Old Vinegar" at Moorfields in London and a booth operated nearby run by a certain "Long Charles" Rimmington. Figg himself ran an annual programme at Southwark Fair every September, closing the show himself with an exhibition of all his fighting skills

James Figg continued to take part in competitive bouts, but in 1724 at Gravesend, Kent, Figg was, according to some sources, beaten by Ned Sutton who was known as the "The Pipemaker". Whether this was for the Champion of England title is unclear, however Figg soon reversed that result by beating Sutton the next year. Those same records also show that he fought Sutton another three times, all in London at his Oxford Road boxing booth, a couple of exhibitions against him in 1727, then once again the same year for the title of Champion of England, which Figg retained.

Although only fighting spasmodically after this in informal fights or exhibitions, he kept the championship until his retirement in 1730, although Figg did participate in an exhibition bout with Jack Broughton in 1733. It is said that during his fighting career James Figg took part in over 270 fights only losing the once to Ned Sutton.

Later, after he had retired and because he rubbed shoulders over the years with aristocracy and the nobility, who generally patronized his fights and exhibitions, James Figg was honoured by being made a Yeoman of the Guard. He continued to socialize with noblemen, the Prince of Wales and other members of the Royal Family for the rest of his life.

He died after suffering a bout of pneumonia in 1734, leaving his wife and several children in comfortable circumstances after eventually ending up a rich man.

Although a crude, illiterate bruiser by today's standards, James Figg will best be remembered as the man who established the art of self defence and boxing in England.

1719
Claimed the Championship of England.

1720-1723

Timothy Buck, Oxford Road, London	W		
Tom Stokes, Oxford Road, London	W		
Bill Flanders, Oxford Road, London	W		
Chris Clarkson, Oxford Road, London	W		30min.

All the fights above were billed at the time as for the Championship of England.

1724

Ned Sutton, Gravesend, Kent	L	

Lost the Championship.

1725

Ned Sutton, Oxford Road, London	W	

Regained the Championship.

1727

Ned Sutton, Oxford Road, London	EX		60min.
Ned Sutton, Oxford Road, London	EX		60min.
Ned Sutton, Oxford Road, London	W	8r.	10min.

Retained the Championship.

1730
Officially retired from fighting.

1733

Jack Broughton, Oxford Road, London	EX	3r.

Tom Pipes
(Claimed the Championship 1730-1734)

Born: c.1702   Died: Unknown

"The Claimant"

Not much is known about Tom Pipes (real name Thomas Allen) apart from the fact that he weighed about 172lbs. was about 5' 10" tall and although not the strongest of men he was a fast and clever, hard hitting fighter, whose main tactic was to target the head of an opponent. He was also a man who could take punishment as well as dish it out and was as game and courageous as any other pugilist of that era.

Pipes became a student of James Figg and when Figg retired in 1730 neither highly rated George Taylor or Jack Broughton made a claim on his title. Tom Pipes did and it was generally accepted in prize fighting circles, apart from Bill Gretting, who disputed Pipes claim, after first losing to Pipes in 1729 and then beating him. They met again in 1730, where first Gretting again beat Pipes and then later in the same year lost to him. Pipes lost to Gretting once again in 1732 but in 1733 beat him twice and although all these fights were claimed to be for the right to be Champion of England, it is doubtful if they were. However as no one else stepped forward or were too afraid at the time to face them to claim the title, Pipes and Gretting probably decided they were the best around according to who won and assumed the honour themselves!

As it turned out Jack Broughton then stepped in to easily beat Pipes and Gretting twice each in 1734, putting beyond all doubt as to whom the real champion was.

Tom Pipes only had one more recorded fight, a draw, against Jack (James) Taylor which is unfortunately undated. It is rumoured that had Pipes not led a life of debauchery he could have won a lot more fights.

Circa 1729

Bill Gretting	L
Bill Gretting	W

6

1730

Claimed the Championship of England after Figg retired. Bill Gretting disputed this claim.
Bill Gretting   L
Claimed as for the Championship of England.
Bill Gretting   W
Claimed as for the Championship of England.

1732

Bill Gretting   L
Claimed as for the Championship of England.
Bob Whitaker   L

1733

Bill Gretting   W
Claimed as for the Championship of England.
Bill Gretting   W
Claimed as for the Championship of England.

1734

Jack Broughton   L
Claimed as for the Championship of England.
Jack Broughton   L
Claimed as for the Championship of England.

Undated
JackTaylor   D

Bill Gretting
(Claimed the Championship 1730-1733)

Born: c.1703   Died: Unknown

"The Claimant"

Nothing of Bill Gretting's early life is known and the only personal statistics we have about him are that he stood about 5' 11" in height, weighed around 180lbs. and that he was a big, strong man although slow and ponderous with little scientific skill. Bigger and stronger than his main antagonist Tom Pipes he was reputed to lack the courage of Pipes throughout his ring career. However he was a powerful puncher with his target mainly the stomach.

After winning and then losing to Tom Pipes in 1729 and then winning and losing to him several more times from 1730-1733, being severely beaten by Pipes in their two fights in 1733, he always claimed to be the Champion of England when he won. He was easily beaten by Jack Broughton twice in 1734, but like many other fighters who thought they were invincible and so did not pay too much attention to fitness combined with heavy drinking, he found with Broughton that it did not work.

He also lost to Hammersmith Jack in 1730, who immediately retired and so Gretting immediately reclaimed the title. He also lost to George Taylor another crude bruiser but a more superior one in 1736 and after that there are no records of his continuance in the prize ring.

Circa 1729

Tom Pipes	W
Tom Pipes	L

1730

Tom Pipes	W

Claimed as for the Championship of England.

Hammersmith Jack	L

Claimed as for the Championship of England. Hammersmith Jack retired so Gretting reclaimed the title.

Tom Pipes	L

Claimed as for the Championship of England.

1732

Tom Pipes	W

Claimed as for the Championship of England.

1733

Tom Pipes   L
Claimed as for the Championship of England.
Tom Pipes   L
Claimed as for the Championship of England.

1734

Jack Broughton   L
Claimed as for the Championship of England.
Jack Broughton   L
Claimed as for the Championship of England.

1736

George Taylor   L
Claimed as for the Championship of England.

George Taylor
(Champion of England 1734-1736)

Born: 1716   Died: 1758

"The Barber"

Born in Norwich, Norfolk George Taylor was a strong but crude fighter, a hard hitter and an expert in performing the cross buttock on his opponents, but was found to be an untrustworthy and not very courageous prize fighter. He stood about 5' 8" and weighed around 190lbs. and when Figg died in 1734 he claimed the Championship of England, but only because James Figg had nominated him as his successor. He also obtained Figg's amphitheatre where other boxers such as Jack Broughton, Prince Boswell, George Stevenson, Tom Smallwood, Buckhorse, Tom Pipes and Bill Gretting all took part in fights and gave exhibitions, just as Figg had done. Between 1730 and 1734 Tom Pipes and Bill Gretting fought each other seven times with Bill Gretting winning four and Tom Pipes three and both claiming it was for the Championship of England.

Taylor then built his own amphitheatre and after beating many of the top fighters claimed he was the Champion of England; however Taylor came unstuck when he was demolished by Jack Broughton in twenty minutes in 1736. He reclaimed the championship when Broughton retired in 1741 and later that year he easily beat the clever gypsy king, Prince Boswell in London in four rounds, because although Boswell had all the skills and had beaten Taylor two years earlier, the one thing he lacked was even less courage than Taylor.

In 1743 Jack Broughton opened his own amphitheatre, returned to the ring and reclaimed the Championship that he had never lost to Taylor and a year or so later George Taylor was forced to close his amphitheatre down and embarrassingly be employed by Broughton, taking part in many fights against all-comers. In January 1750, in London, Taylor defeated Jack Slack in seventeen rounds and in April of that same year he reclaimed the Championship again when Slack refused a return fight, but as Slack had already beaten Jack Broughton for the actual title just before Taylor's claim, George Taylor's shout did not hold water.

In 1751 Taylor retired as a pugilist and became landlord of the Fountain Inn, Deptford in London; however he came out of retirement to beat Tom Faulkner twice in 1757 but also lost to Faulkner in August 1758 in twenty six rounds. Faulkner did make a rather weak claim for the title after this fight because of Slack's inactivity, but Jack Slack was still the truly recognized champion by the Fancy, so although Faulkner was a really useful pugilist he was never really recognized as being the champion.

The defeat by Faulkner was George Taylor's last fight and it was only a few months later in December of 1758 when he passed away aged 42.

1734
Claimed the Championship of England after Figg's death.

1736
Jack Broughton, Tottenham Court Rd, London	L		20min.

Lost the Championship.
Bill Gretting	W		

1739
Benjamin "Gypsy" Boswell, Tottenham Court Road, London	L		16min. £100

1741
Reclaimed the Championship after Broughton's retirement.
Benjamin "Gypsy" Boswell, Tottenham Court Rd, London	W	4r.	135min.

Claimed as for the Championship of England.

1743
Sailor Field, Tottenham Court Rd, London	W		

Broughton came out of retirement and reclaimed the championship that he had never lost in the ring.

1744-1750
Met all comers and apparently undefeated, however these fights were not recorded.

1750
Jack Slack, Oxford Street, London	W	17r.	25min.	+purse

1751
Jack Slack	W		16min.

1754
Tom Faulkner	W	

11

1755
Tom Faulkner   W

1758
Tom Faulkner, St. Albans, Herts.   L   26r.   75min.   400gns.
Claimed as for the Championship of England but was not recognized.

Jack Broughton
(Champion of England 1734-1750)

Born: 1704   Died: 1789

"The Father of Boxing"

Running away from a broken home at the age of twelve to Bristol, Jack Broughton grew up into a powerful, muscular man who stood just less than 6' 0" tall and weighing about 196lbs. Broughton was described as having an even temperament, a generous disposition combined with intelligence and wit. He worked as a waterman and impressed the great James Figg who had taken his troupe of booth fighters to the West Country. Figg offered Broughton a place at his boxing academy in London and Broughton readily accepted, winning all his contests in the capital.

Before James Figg died he nominated George Taylor "The Barber" as his succeeding champion and proprietor of his amphitheatre, but Tom Pipes and Bill Gretting, both distinguished pugilists in their own right, also laid claim as Champion of England. Tom Pipes had fought two back to back wins over Bill Gretting, but Broughton beat both of them several times between 1734 and 1736 and so claimed to be the rightful champion. However George Taylor still recognized himself as champion, this soon changed however when the powerful blows of Broughton rendered him unconscious in 20 minutes at the Tottenham Court Road amphitheatre in 1736.

Jack Broughton is best remembered for his skills as a fighter and the innovations he brought to the free-for-all fighting that preceded boxing as we know it today. In 1743 he devised what is known as *Broughton's Rules* which refined pugilism to a certain extent by cutting out some of the street fighting, anything goes style of boxing which had prevailed up until then and so pugilism bestowed on him the title of "The Father of Boxing". Perhaps he thought he was repaying a debt he owed to George Stevenson "The Coachman" who died after they had fought a tough and unrelenting battle in April 1741. Stevenson clung to life for a month before dying of the injuries sustained during their fight. Broughton took Stevenson's death badly and temporarily retired after this fight, only to return in 1742, winning against Jack James and Prince Boswell at the Oxford Road amphitheatre. Between 1744 and 1746 he carried on his winning ways against William Willis, the redoubtable Thomas Smallwood and "Chicken" Harris. In 1747 he fought and beat the capable "Sailor" Field, all these fights claimed to be for the Championship of England.

The Duke of Cumberland became Broughton's patron and his career really took off socially because through the duke he was introduced to famous people of the day and toured Europe with him as well, meeting various heads of state, but these favours were quickly withdrawn in 1750 when Broughton lost the title of Champion of England to Jack Slack, with the duke losing heavily in a wager backing Broughton to win. With all the socializing involved during these years Broughton had grown soft and unfit, plus the fact he was forty six when he took on Slack who was twenty nine. Broughton probably underestimated Slack, knowing him to be a crude bruiser and never bothered about training too much for a contest against a man who was just a known bully. Even so, after having the better of Slack in the opening rounds Broughton was suddenly blinded by a sucker punch from Slack and was forced to retire after less than 30 minutes of fighting.

Broughton had a fascinating life outside of boxing, as in 1730, when he was already a successful fighter he used his old skills as a waterman to win a prestigious rowing event on the Thames in London and for a man who was in the tough and brutal career of bare knuckle prize fighting, outside the ring and after he had retired, Broughton took as much joy from tending flowers as he did boxing.

When he was in the Duke of Cumberland's good books the duke bestowed on Broughton the title of Yeoman of the Guard, a title he kept until he died. In fact after he had retired from boxing, the contacts he had made socially, along with the amphitheatre he had purchased in 1738 as a boxing academy and which he transformed into a furniture market, made him enough money to dabble in stocks and shares, which increased his fortune even further.

On his death at home in Walcott Place, Lambeth in London in 1789, Broughton is apparently reputed to have amassed a considerable fortune of about £7,000, a considerable sum in those days, through boxing and his other business adventures which left his family in very comfortable circumstances.

1725-1732
Broughton took part in many turn ups and minor fights in and around Bristol. His first recorded fight was against an unknown bully who he beat in 10 rounds.

1733
James Figg, Oxford Street, London   EX

1734-1736
Tom Pipes   W
Bill Gretting   W
Claimed as for the Championship of England. He fought these two several times.
George Taylor, Tottenham Court Road,
    London   W   20min.
Recognized as for the Championship of England.

1737
"Buckhorse" John Smith (Buckhorse), London   W
Retained the Championship.

1741
George Stevenson, Tottenham Court Road,
    London   W   4r.   39min.
Retained the Championship.

1742
Jack James, Oxford Street, London   W
Retained the Championship.
Benjamin "Gypsy" Boswell, London   W
Retained the Championship.

1744-1746
William Willis, London   W
Retained the Championship.
Tom Smallwood, Oxford Street, London   W
Retained the Championship.
"Chicken" Harris, Oxford Street, London   W
Retained the Championship.

1747
Sailor Field, London   W
Retained the Championship.

1750
Jack Slack, Oxford Street, London   L   4r.   14min.   £600
Lost the Championship.

London Prize Ring Rules
known as Broughton's Rules (1743)

(To be observed on all battles on the stage)

(1) That a square of a yard be chalked in the middle of the stage, and on every fresh set-to after a fall, or being parted from the rails, each second is to bring his man to the side of the square, and place him opposite to the other, and till they are fairly set-to at the lines, it shall not be lawful for one to strike at the other.

(2) That, in order to prevent any disputes, the time a man lies after a fall, if the second does not bring his man to the side of the square, within the space of half a minute, he shall be deemed a beaten man.

(3) That in every main battle, no person whatever shall be upon the stage, except the principals and their seconds, the same rule to be observed in bye-battles, except that in the latter, Mr. Broughton is allowed to be upon the stage to keep decorum, and to assist gentlemen in getting to their places, provided always he does not interfere in the battle; and whoever pretends to infringe these rules to be turned immediately out of the house. Everybody is to quit the stage as soon as the principals are stripped, before the set-to.

(4) That no man be deemed beaten, unless he fails coming up to the line in the limited time, or that his own second declares him beaten. No second is to be allowed to ask his man's adversary any questions, or advise him to give out.

(5) That in bye-battles, the winning man to have two-thirds of the money given, which shall be publicly divided upon the stage, notwithstanding any private agreements to the contrary.

(6) That to prevent disputes, in every main battle the principals shall, on coming on the stage, choose from among the gentlemen present two umpires, who shall absolutely decide all disputes that may arise about the battle; and if the two umpires cannot agree, the said umpires to choose a third, who is to determine it.

(7) That no people is to hit his adversary when he is down, or seize him by the ham, the breeches, or any part below the waist: a man on his knees to be reckoned down.

Jack Slack
(Champion of England 1750-1760)

Born: 1721   Died: 1768

"The Norfolk Butcher"

Jack Slack was alleged to have been James Figg's grandson and was described as a swaggering bully boy, who, after beating an unfit Jack Broughton for the Championship of England in 1750 could have gone on to better things but didn't, as he is believed to have fixed several of his fights, which was quite a common practice then.

A heavily built man who weighed about 196lb. but only standing about 5' 8", he had little skill, although possessing great strength, hitting power, stamina and courage. Born at Thorpe in Norfolk, Slack was a butcher by trade with his own business and later came marriage which eventually bore him two sons. After several wins locally including victories against Thomas Hawksley and Bob Smith twice, Slack was recognized as the Norfolk Champion and eventually set out for fame and fortune in London where he fought the clever Ned Hunt, winning in eight rounds, although Ned Hunt, who at about 118lb. and 5' 5" tall was so much smaller than Slack and was forced many times to take on heavier men just to get a fight. Slack also beat the tough James "Sailor" Field in February 1749, and then followed that up with a win over the colourful gypsy, Benjamin "Prince" Boswell, but then lost to the superiority of George Taylor in January 1750.

After challenging the recognized champion, Jack Broughton, while attending the Hounslow Races, they met in April 1750 in London, the result being that after four rounds, an apparently unfit and overweight Broughton, caught by a sucker punch which temporarily blinded him, could not continue. After this fight the new Champion of England was involved in reputedly fixed fights, although it has to be said he did hold the title for 10 years, albeit under highly dubious circumstances, but he still attracted the patronage of the Duke of Cumberland, who disassociated himself from Broughton as soon as he was defeated by Slack, having betted heavily and lost on Broughton to win.

Jack Slack set up and ran a booth in London and when business was slow, or when he was resting between contests he took his collection of fighters on the road, touring the length and breadth of the land and helping to establish Bristol as a major fight centre in the process.

After beating Broughton to gain the title of Champion of England Slack lost again to George Taylor in February 1751, although it seems this fight was apparently not for the title. He then went on to beat George Lee and Thomas Faulkner in February and May 1752 respectively and then lost his next fight to Elias Goddard in November of that year. He beat a French giant called Pettit in Harleston on the Norfolk/Suffolk border in July 1754, who, when he was losing, decided to run away from the ring! Slack also knocked out Cornelius "King Cole" Harris, a miner by trade (and rumoured murderer), at Kingswood, near Bristol in March 1755. When Harris had recovered he apparently rushed after Slack in an attempt to murder him as well! He then defeated a certain Jack Moreton (or Morton), apparently a farmhand, in October 1759 at Acton Wells, just outside London, in what is described as his first recognized championship fight since his defeat of Broughton. He lost his title in June 1760 to William "The Nailer" Stevens when he was knocked out in four rounds lasting 27 minutes and being unable to be revived by his seconds in the half minute allowed.

With this defeat Slack retired and returned to his old trade of butcher, apparently running a prosperous enterprise in Covent Garden, London until his death in 1768.

1743
After beating three local opponents he was recognized as the Champion of Norfolk.

Tom Auger, New Buckenham, Norfolk	W			
Jack James, London	W		4min.	
Tom Smallwood, London	L			

1744

Bob Smith, East Anglia	W	18r.	45min.	
Bob Smith, Framlingham, Suffolk	W		20min.	80gns+purse

1745-1746
Slack won several contests on the provincial circuit.

Ned Palmer	W	6r.
Jack Kenny	W	4r.
Bill Wass	W	16r.
George Pierce	W	14r.
Tom Hawksley	W	

1747

George Taylor	L		36min.
George Taylor, London	L		

1748

Ned Hunt, London	W	8r.	40min.	£100
Benjamin Boswell, London	W			

1749

James Field, Oxford Street, London	W		92min.

1750

George Taylor, London	L	17r.	25min.	+purse
Jack Broughton, Oxford Street, London	W	4r.	14min.	£600

Won the Championship of England.

1751

George Taylor, London	L		16min.

1752

George Lea, London	W		3min.
Tom Faulkner, London	W		27min.
Elias Goddard	L		

1754

Monsieur Petit, Harleston, Norfolk	W	7r.	25min.

Retained the Championship. (Other records date this fight as taken place in 1751).

1755

John Harris, Barton Hundreds, Norfolk	W		6min.	
Cornelius Harris, Kingswood, Bristol	W	5r.	20min.	200gns.

Retained the Championship.

1759

Jack Moreton, Old Oak Common, Acton Wells, London	W		35 min.	£100

Retained the Championship.

1760

Bill Stevens, Haymarket, London	L	4r.	27min.	200gns.

Lost the Championship.

William Stevens
(Champion of England 1760-1761)

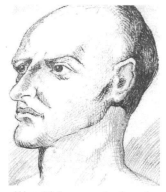

Born: 1736   Died: 1794

"The Nailer"

William Stevens was probably just as shady a character as Jack Slack although apparently he could have been a top class pugilist if it wasn't for the fact that he thought more of making a fast buck than boxing, or in other words if he was offered more money for losing than winning then Stevens was up for it! He fought Jack Slack for the so called title in June 1760 at Jack Broughton's academy, the Tennis Court in the Haymarket, the first great pugilistic event in London for ten years since Slack had beaten Broughton.

William Stevens was the son of a female blacksmith and was born at Lye in Staffordshire, and grew up to be a well-built man of about 5' 10" and weighing about 190lb. He came to be patronized by the then Duke of York when the duke witnessed his impressive win, by a knockout after thirteen rounds, of the tough Jacob Taplin, a coal heaver, at Marylebone Fields, London in February 1760. In a contest in which Taplin was ahead in the first part of the fight, Stevens rallied to finish Taplin off with a terrific body blow and then several more violent punches.

His meeting with Slack for the title in June 1760 began with the early advantage to Stevens when he felled Slack with a body punch; however he was generally outwrestled and tried to keep the fight at long range to avoid the champion's famed rabbit punch from being used on him. He had to take some of these until, in round four, he caught Slack with a terrific punch to the head, then threw him over his leg, cracking Slack's head on the floor. With his seconds unable to revive Slack in the allocated half minute allowed, William Stevens took the title of Champion of England. The Duke of York who had bet heavily on Slack now lost another substantial purse for the second time on a fighter whose patronage he had chosen and so this time he immediately changed hats to become an anti-boxing supporter!

As already stated Stevens was another untrustworthy character and within nine months of winning the title he took a dive against George

Meggs, in March 1761 in London, giving up all too easily after 17 minutes. Jack Slack was probably behind the fix, making it worthwhile to throw the fight, which Stevens admitted to shortly after as being rigged. He was now held in disgrace by the Fancy and decided to retire as he could not get fights because of the debacle with Meggs. There is no trace of him fighting for eight years and on his return to the ring he was only fighting for paltry purses or for nothing at all. He beat an Irishman, John McGuire, in 20 minutes, at Bloomsbury Fields, London, in July 1769, lost to an inexperienced Bill Turner in 130 minutes a month later and then lost again in 10 minutes to Harry Sellers in June 1778 for a purse of only £25 at the age of 42. He died penniless in London in 1794 at the age of 58.

1756-1759
Bill Stevens won several unrecorded minor fights.

1760

Jacob Taplin, Marylebone, London	W	13r.	30 min.	
Jack Slack, Haymarket, London	W	4r.	27 min.	200gns.

Won the Championship of England.

1761

George Meggs, Haymarket, London	L	17 min.	£400

Lost the Championship.

1769

John McGuire, Montague House, Bloomsbury, London	W	20 min.	20gns.
Bill Turner, Hyde Park, London	L	130 min.	£10

1778

Harry Sellers	L	10 min.	£25

For the Championship of England.

George Meggs
(Champion of England 1761-1762)

Born: 1735   Died: Unknown

"The Collier"

Born in Bristol around about 1735 Meggs stood about 5' 8" and weighed around 175lbs. and although he was a strong and powerful man, because of his early employment as a collier, he was also slow and ponderous and he can only be classed as a very average prize fighter. This was in fact the start of several years of continuing mediocrity in pugilism in which the championship swapped hands several times amongst average or below average thugs. Because of this shortage of good quality fighters many of the nobility withdrew their money and support through lack of interest.

Meggs reputedly bought the title from Bill Stevens when they met at the Haymarket, London in 1761, winning in 17 minutes. Stevens openly boasted that he was paid to lose to the inferior Meggs and with the rather dubious and shady Jack Slack also allegedly involved, then this is probably true.

George Meggs lost the title straight away against the also very ordinary George Milsom the following year at Calne, Wiltshire in what surprisingly turned out to be a well contested and evenly fought fight lasting 40 minutes. Not happy with the outcome, Meggs challenged Milsom to a return later in the year and at Lansdowne near Bath, where Meggs was once again the loser. Meggs last reported fight was against Bill Darts at Shepton Mallet, Somerset and yet another defeat before he disappeared from the boxing scene.

1761

Bill Stevens, Haymarket, London (fixed fight?)	W	17min.	£400

Won the Championship of England.

1762

George Milsom, Calne, Wilts.	L	40min.	£100
George Milsom, Lansdowne, Bath	L		

Both these fights were billed as for the Championship of England.

1764

Bill Darts, Shepton Mallet, Somerset	L

George Milsom
(Champion of England 1762-1765)

Born: 1740   Died: Unknown

"The Baker"

Not much is known about George Milsom apart from the fact that he was born in Bath around 1740 and found employment as a baker. His fighting weight was about 182lbs. and he was about 5' 11" tall. Reputed to be strong and courageous he apparently never possessed any great boxing skills to go with his strength. Nothing is known of any earlier fights, his first recorded fight was his contest against George Meggs at Calne, Wiltshire in 1762 earning him the title of Champion of England which he retained a month later against the same man. He then beat George Meggs brother Parfit the next year at Beckhampton, Wiltshire, before losing the title to Tom Juchau at St. Albans, Hertfordshire in 1765.

Like his fellow West Country man, George Meggs before him, Milsom also only fought once outside the West Country according to the records, possibly suggesting that maybe these fights were fixes.

1762

George Meggs, Calne, Wilts.	W	40min.	£100
Won the Championship of England.			
George Meggs, Lansdowne, Bath	W		
Retained the Championship.			

1763

Parfit Meggs, Beckhampton, Wilts.	W	
Retained the Championship.		

1765

Tom Juchau, St. Albans, Herts.	L	70min.
Lost the Championship.		

Tom Juchau
(Champion of England 1765-1766)

Born: 1740   Died: Unknown

"The Paviour"

Tom Juchau was originally of either German or Swiss nationality and worked as a labourer, laying paving stones. Standing about 5' 10" and weighing close on 188lbs. his prowess as a pugilist seemed good enough at least to the Duke of Richmond, who had enough confidence in him to be his backer.

Although very little is known about him he is rated as a first class fighter who done his best to be matched against the best pugilists in this period, although these were few and far between. He probably won his fair share of fights, but like so many fighters of this period the results have either been lost in the mists of time or went unrecorded.

His first recorded fight against Charles Coant in June 1764 at Guildford, Surrey was classed as a good even fight with Coant, a butcher by trade, who was for the first half hour the better man, but when Juchau delivered a powerful body blow it changed the course of the fight. Within minutes from receiving that punch Coant was forced to give in. When he fought George Milsom for the title in August 1765 at St. Albans, Hertfordshire in another well contested fight, Juchau was the better man throughout the fight although it is reported that Milsom did not disgrace himself.

The next year was Tom Juchau's last as champion when he lost in an epic contest of 17 rounds against Bill Darts at Guildford, Surrey.

1764

Charles Coant, Guildford, Surrey	W		47min.	purse

1765

George Milsom, St. Albans, Herts.	W		70min.	

Won the Championship of England.

1766

Bill Darts, Guildford, Surrey	L	17r.	40min.	1,000gns.

Lost the Championship.

Bill Darts
(Champion of England 1766-1771)

Born: 1741   Died: 1781

"The Dyer"

Born in 1741 in Spitalfields, which is now in the east end of London, Bill Darts was about 5' 10" in height and weighed in the region of 188lbs.-190lbs. He was described as being a good, tricky, skilful and hard hitting fighter; however his stamina and courage was suspect at times.

He first entered the ring in June 1764 against Parfit Meggs, the brother of former champion, George Meggs, at Shepton Mallett, Somerset, beating Meggs in a fight lacking in details. Bill Darts fight with Tom Juchau in May 1766 at Guildford, Surrey was a tough affair with the fight going one way and then the other, but Darts proved victorious in the end with Tom Juchau failing to make it for the eighteenth round. In 1767 he continued his winning ways, defeating a West Country bargeman known only by the name of Doggett at Melksham, Wiltshire in six rounds taking an hour and then beating a butcher known only as Swansey, in 15 minutes at Epping Forest, Essex.

The championship contest with Tom Lyons at Kingston-upon-Thames, London in June 1769 was also another tough fight for Bill Darts and although for the first 25 minutes he was beginning to get on top, Lyons came back strongly to beat him and after 45 minutes was acclaimed as the winner. Although Darts lost the championship, Lyons either didn't want to meet Darts again or was finished with prize fighting, immediately refusing to meet him in a return match and retired, so allowing Darts to reclaim the title. Bill Darts was another fighter that was backed by the Duke of Richmond. After the fight against Lyons his next fight was with the celebrated Steve "Death" Oliver at Putney, London which Darts won in twenty seven rounds.

The fight in which he lost the title to Peter Corcoran in May 1771 at Epsom Races was considered a fix by some at the time. It was a total farce lasting just one minute and thought to be instigated by the

26

famous man of the turf of that era, Captain O'Kelly, although no evidence of a fix was ever proved.

1764

Parfit Meggs, Shepton Mallet, Somerset	W			

1766

Tom Juchau, Guildford, Surrey	W	17r.	40min.	1,000gns.

Won the Championship of England.

1767

Bargeman Doggett, Melksham, Wilts.	W	6r.	60min.	£100
Butcher Swansey, Epping Forest	W		15min.	100gns.

Both fights billed as for the Championship of England.

1769

Tom Lyons, Kingston-upon-Thames, London	L		45min.	

Lost the championship but reclaimed it as Lyons refused a return fight and retired.

1770

Steve Oliver, Putney	W		27min.	

Claimed as for the Championship of England.

1771

Peter Corcoran, Epsom Races	L	1r.	7min.	£200

Lost the Championship.

Tom Lyons
(Champion of England 1769)

Born: 1740   Died: Unknown

"The Waterman"

Tom Lyons was reputed to be a very strong and tough individual, a powerful hitter and possessing a tremendous capacity for taking punishment, however, even with all these attributes he was still only recognized as a crude street brawler in terms of skill. He stood 6' 0" tall and weighed up to 196lbs. but was ponderous and slow in movement.

Nothing is known of any previous fight before the championship fight with Darts; however he probably worked his way up a list of lesser known pugilists to place himself in the position as a contender. His victory against Bill Darts for the title in June 1769 at Kingston-upon-Thames, although a tough fight by two equally matched fighters, was a shock and totally unexpected, as Darts was the firm favourite to win. For the first 25 minutes Darts carried the fight to Lyons and was having it all his own way, but then began to tire and Tom Lyons superior stamina then took over to carry him to victory in a bruising contest.

As his nickname suggests he probably worked the barges on the canals, but apart from that nothing more is known about him and no more fights are recorded in his name.

Prior to 1768
Tom Lyons beat many unrecorded opponents in many street fights and turn ups in and around London.

1769
Bill Darts, Kingston-upon-Thames, London   W   45min.
Won the Championship of England.

Peter Corcoran
(Champion of England 1771-1776)

Born: 1740   Died: c.1784

"The Irish Champion"

Peter Corcoran was born in 1740 at Athy, County Kildare in Ireland and was thought to be involved in the prize fighting scene in the Emerald Isle. In the early 1760's he fled Ireland to escape the law to England after it was alleged that he killed a local man in a drunken brawl over a woman and never returned to Ireland. He first settled in Birmingham where he worked as a coalman, then to Portsmouth as a sailor. It was at this time that Corcoran first became involved in prize fighting in England and because of several successes locally, he moved to London. He also settled in as landlord of the Black Horse Inn, Dyer Street, East London and as his fighting career prospered he moved to larger premises, The Blakeney Arms at St. Martin's Lane, London. However this business was not a success and he suffered major financial losses.

He was a strong, hard hitting two fisted fighter standing at just an inch under 6' 0" and weighing 186lbs. but apparently with very little boxing skill and apparently would throw a fight if needed. In London he attracted the attention of Colonel Dennis Kelly, another Irishman, who was a noted racehorse owner and gambler and Kelly became Corcoran's sponsor, arranging training and prize fights for him.

Corcoran's first major fight was in September 1769, at Hyde Park in London where he easily defeated Bill Turner. At the time Turner was considered one of the leading fighters in England and over the next year Corcoran met and defeated three other leading contenders, namely Tom Dalton, Jack Davis and Bob Smiler "The Bricklayer", all these fights being held at Longfields in London, which now lies behind the British Museum. Following these victories, Corcoran challenged the then champion Bill Darts. Darts faced Corcoran for the title fight at Epsom Downs racecourse, Surrey in May 1771, the fight being held after the Epsom Derby. The fight was the shortest championship title fight on record, Corcoran knocking Darts out in less than a minute. The fight is shrouded in controversy, as

Corcoran's backer, Colonel Dennis Kelly won a very large wager on the outcome of the fight and it is rumoured that Darts was bribed to take a dive, resulting in the fact that Darts was ostracized from the fighting fraternity after this.

Corcoran held the title for five years and during this time he defended it on numerous occasions, although many believe that a lot of these contests could also have been fixed. The only leading contender he faced in these title fights was Sam Peters and this fight was staged at Waltham Abbey, Essex in 1774, where Corcoran emerged an easy winner in just three rounds over his supposedly highly rated challenger; again suggestions of a fix are understandable.

Corcoran lost the title in October 1776, when he was by defeated by Harry Sellers the fight being held at Staines in Middlesex; Corcoran was the betting favourite to retain his title, however he was defeated in a contest which lasted eighteen rounds. It is highly probable that he threw this fight as well because before the fight Corcoran was in severe financial difficulties, after the fight these debts mysteriously disappeared! The Sellers fight was Corcoran's last contest; there is no further mention of Corcoran engaging in any further bouts.

There are no details of his death, other than that he died in poverty and his funeral expenses had to be paid for by public subscription.

1765-1768
Corcoran won numerous unrecorded fights in Ireland and was eventually recognized as the Irish Champion.

1769
Bill Turner, Hyde Park, London   W   20min.   £40
A newspaper report at the time states Turner the winner.

1770
Bob Smiler, London   W
Tom Dalton, London   W
Joe Davis, London   W

1771
Bill Darts, Epsom Races (fixed fight?)   W   1r.   7min.   £200
Won the Championship of England.

1774
Sam Peters, Waltham Abbey, Essex (fixed fight?) W   3r.   15min.
Retained the Championship.

1776
Harry Sellers, Staines (fixed fight?)   L   18r.   38min.   200gns.
Lost the Championship.

Harry Sellers
(Champion of England 1776-1785)

Born: 1753   Died: Unknown

"The West Countryman"

Harry Sellers was born in Bristol and was the classic bully, because when somebody stood up to him, he quit. He had one secret weapon however, because when the going got tough in the ring he had a habit of falling down, cunningly throwing a punch as he went. Sellers was a well-built fighter, just under 6' 0" in height and weighing around 175lbs. He gained the championship from Peter Corcoran in an allegedly fixed fight at Staines, Middlesex in October 1776. Corcoran knocked Sellers across the ring with his very first punch and from then on Sellers fought very defensively for a while, making Corcoran do all the chasing and allowing him to run out of steam, before mounting his own attack on his opponent and forcing Corcoran to submit.

Sellers first recorded fight was against Parfitt Meggs at Shepton Mallet, Somerset in June 1774, where he was the victor and for the next year he involved himself in several minor contests which have gone unrecorded. As champion, Sellers fought and beat the experienced and popular Joe Hood twice, both fights being held within a month of each other in June and July of 1777, the first one in which Hood showed great courage and determination before admitting defeat after half an hour of fighting, at Ascot Racecourse, Berkshire, the other being at Ipswich, Norfolk. He then defended the title again to beat George "The Nailer" Stevens in June 1778, winning in 10 minutes.

In September 1779 he took on an Irish boatswain, Duggan Fearns outside the Crown Inn at Slough, Berkshire. Nothing is known of Fearns being a pugilist, but Sellers fell over at the first half decent blow thrown by Fearns and refused to carry on, so it was all over in 90 seconds! Duggan Fearns, with no interest in defending the championship was never heard of again, presumably returning to his seafaring ways and boasting as being the Champion of England!

Sellers last fight was against another Irishman called William Harvey in a field near a pub called the Black Dog at Holywell Mount, Shoreditch, London. Sellers apparently in a drunken state insulted Harvey inside the pub thinking that when he stated who he was the Irishman would back down, but he didn't and called for Sellers to step outside to settle their differences. Sellers ended up well beaten in just over a quarter of an hour and after this set-to Sellers disappears into the mists of time, as nothing more is known about him.

1773-1775
Sellers won several fights that went largely unrecorded.

1776
Peter Corcoran, Staines (fixed fight?)   W   18r.   38min.   200gns.
Won the Championship of England.

1777
Joe Hood, Ascot Heath, Berks.   W   30min.   £100
Joe Hood, Ipswich, Norfolk   W
Retained the Championship.

1778
Bill Stevens, *unknown venue*   W   10min.   £50
Retained the Championship.

1779
Duggan Fearns, Slough (fixed fight?)   L   1r.   1½min.   £50
Lost the championship. (Fearns never defended title so Sellers reclaimed the championship).
Sellers fight with Jack Harris in 1780 could be the one above, making Fearns and Harris the
same person.

1785
William Harvey, Holloway, London (turn up)   L   20min.   13gns.

Duggan Fearns
(Champion of England 1779)

Born: c.1754   Died: Unknown

Nothing is known about Duggan or Jack Fearns apart from the fact that he was probably Irish and apparently a boatswain, who, after beating Sellers and removing the Championship of England title from him, disappeared never to resurface again in the annals of pugilism. He was described at the time as being 5' 10" tall and weighing about 182lbs.

The fight was held outside the Crown Inn, Slough and many believe it was a fixed fight, because although he was probably a strong and tough bruiser, Fearns should never have really stood a chance against a seasoned professional, yet he knocked Sellers out in only 90 seconds! Because Fearns disappeared immediately after the fight Sellers later reclaimed the title when everyone realized the new champion was nowhere to be found.

This happily ended the so called Black Period of the prize ring which had started with George Meggs in 1761. Because of the combination of poor quality pugilists and shady customers inside and outside the ring, interest in prize fighting nearly died. With the advent of Tom Johnson arriving on the scene interest was revived in prize fighting and with it started a golden era of pugilism.

1779
Harry Sellers, Slough (fixed fight?)   W   1r.   1½min.   £50
Won the Championship of England.

Tom Johnson
(Champion of England 1787-1791)

Born: 1750   Died: 1797

Tom Johnson arrived at a time when bare knuckle prize fighting was at an all-time low and made the sport respectable again by taking part in some memorable contests. Standing only about 5' 9" tall he weighed in at about a hefty 196lbs. but possessed great skill, courage and coolness. He was also recognized as a patient and determined fighter who never retreated, could switch the angle of his punches and was an adept counter puncher. His real name was Thomas Jackling and he came originally from Derbyshire, but moved to London to find work as a porter in the docks.

His first major win was over Jack Jarvis in June 1783 at Walworth, London in 15 minutes, followed up by another win against someone called the Croydon Drover in 27 minutes, again in London in March 1784. At Blackheath, London he demolished Stephen "Death" Oliver, who was probably by this time in his sixties, as he had worked in the boxing booth of Jack Broughton some thirty to forty years earlier! Johnson had now caught the eye of the Prince of Wales, the future George IV, who became an ardent supporter and who was an enthusiastic supporter of the prize ring anyway.

In 1786 Johnson beat Bill Love, a butcher by trade, followed by Jack Towers both at Barnet, London and in January 1787 after beating Bill Warr in a disappointing fight watched by thousands at Oakingham, (now Wokingham), Berkshire, after Warr jumped out of the ring and disappeared when, after claiming a foul punch by Johnson, he was overruled by the referee. Johnson was now generally recognized as the Champion of England and later that year, in July he beat William Fry at Kingston, London in 30 minutes to confirm the faith of the Fancy. In December 1787 he fought and beat the 6' 4" Irish champion, Michael Ryan at Wradisbury, Buckinghamshire and again, in twelve rounds in a return in February 1789 near Rickmansworth, Hertfordshire. In the first encounter he was lucky not to be disqualified, when, after being floored in the first round, Johnson's second grabbed Ryan, allowing time for Johnson to recover and then go on to win in 30 minutes. The second fight he won decisively in twelve rounds at Rickmansworth, Hertfordshire.

In October 1789 he met the giant Isaac Perrins of Birmingham in a bloody and brutal battle at Banbury in Oxfordshire and making use of continuous body punching wore the game Perrins down in sixty two rounds lasting 75 minutes. In January 1791 he took on big Ben Brain at Wrotham, Kent, again for the championship, but relinquished the title this time when he was battered to defeat in eighteen rounds, after suffering a broken hand and damaged ribs.

Johnson gambled away most of the money he made in the ring, estimated at £5,000 including side bets. With some of the remaining money he took a pub in Lincoln's Inn Field in London and then moved on to one called The Grapes, in Duke Street, London, eventually moving to Ireland and a pub in Cooper's Alley, Dublin, but he was kicked out by the magistrates due to his debts. He died, destitute in County Cork in January 1797 at the age of 47.

1783

Jack Jarvis, Walworth, London	W		15min.	

1784

Croydon Drover, Kennington, London	W		27min.	
Steve "Death" Oliver, Blackheath, London	W		35min.	

1786

Bill Love, Barnet	W		5min.	100gns.
Jack Towers, Barnet	W		15min.	
Irish Coalheaver, Walworth	W		30min.	40gns.

All these fights were billed as for the Championship of England, but this is doubtful.

1787

Bill Warr, Oakingham, Berks.	W		80min.	400gns.
Won the Championship of England.				
Bill Fry, Kingston-upon-Thames, London	W		30min.	100gns.
Retained the Championship.				
Michael Ryan, Wradisbury, Bucks.	W		25min.	200gns.
Retained the Championship.				

1789

Michael Ryan, Rickmansworth, Herts.	W	12r.	33min.	£600
Retained the Championship.				
Isaac Perrins, Banbury, Oxon.	W	62r.	75min.	500gns.
Retained the Championship.				

1791

Ben Brain, Wrotham, Kent	L	18r.	21min.	£1,000
Lost the Championship.				

Benjamin Brain
(Champion of England 1791-1794)

Born: 1753   Died: 1794

"Big Ben"

Born in Bristol, Benjamin Brain became a collier in a local mine. A big lad of somewhere between 6' 0" to 6' 4" Big Ben weighed anywhere between 196lbs.-230lbs. but was very quick and agile considering his size and carried a devastating punch in both hands. His first paid fight when he was 21 in Kingswood, Bristol ended in victory against another collier, Jack Clayton and he then succeeded in defeating another local lad, Bob "Spaniard" Harris also in Kingswood, Bristol. Like so many other men lack of work locally sent Ben to London around 1774, where, for a few years he worked as a coal porter on the Thames Wharf. After a few unrecorded minor skirmishes his first real fight to note in London was against John Boone, the "Fighting Grenadier", in October 1786 at Bloomsbury. A bloody battle evolved with neither man giving an inch and only the ring being torn down by a mob after 30 minutes gave Brain sufficient time to have his swollen eyes lanced and saving him from defeat. After law and order had been restored outside the ring it took just another 10 minutes for Big Ben to render Boone unconscious.

In December 1788, Brain beat Bill Corbally in 20 minutes at Knavestock, Essex and in October 1789 in a bruising battle at Banbury, Oxfordshire he beat Jack Jacombs. In December of that year at Dartford, London he beat Tom Tring in twelve rounds which lasted less than 20 minutes, again having to have his eyes lanced before knocking out an already blinded Tring. In August 1790 at Chapel Row, near Newbury, Berkshire he came up against Bill Hooper "The Tinman" and although the bout was declared a draw after three and a half hours, the fight itself was a farce, due to Hooper running around the ring, spitting and cajoling Brain and falling down every time a punch was either landed or not. In the end darkness insisted it had to be declared a draw and although Hooper was offered a return by Brain he politely and probably sensibly refused.

In January 1791 Brain found the backing for a fight for the championship against the holder Tom Johnson at Wrotham, Kent, a fight which had originally been scheduled for September 1789, but at the time Ben Brain had fallen ill. Both men were undefeated up until then and with an estimated 10,000 spectators in attendance, both men put in a great performance with both taking heavy punishment. However after eighteen rounds Brain caught Johnson firstly, with a terrific blow to the ribs and then another terrible blow to the face and so ending a classic fight, with Ben Brain the new Champion of England. It is said that the punishment that Ben Brain took in this fight, although not seeming to affect him at the time, took its toll afterwards, due to the fact that he never seemed to be in the best of health again after this contest.

Because of a lack of suitable challengers Brain retired but was enticed back into the ring in 1794 with a challenge from William "The Coachman" Wood of Bristol, but big Benjamin Brain suddenly fell ill and died of a liver disease in his rooms at Grays Inn Lane, London in April of that year, still the undefeated Champion of England.

1774

Jack Clayton, Kingswood, Bristol	W			£10
Bob Harris, Kingswood, Bristol	W			

1775-1785
No record available. Probably involved in a few minor fights.

1786

John Boone, Bloomsbury, London	W		40min.	

1788

William Corbally, Knavestock, Essex	W		20min.	50gns.

1789

Jack Jacombs, Banbury, Oxon.	W		85min.	£50
Tom Tring, Dartford, Kent	W	12r.	19min.	20gns.

1790

William Hooper, Newbury, Berks.	D	180r.	210min.	100gns.

1791

Tom Johnson, Wrotham, Kent	W	18r.	21min.	500gns.

Won the Championship of England.

Daniel Mendoza
(Champion of England 1792-1795)

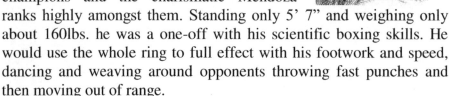

Born: 1764   Died: 1836

"Star of the East"

Born in Aldgate, London in 1764, there have been many great Jewish fighters and champions and the charismatic Mendoza ranks highly amongst them. Standing only 5' 7" and weighing only about 160lbs. he was a one-off with his scientific boxing skills. He would use the whole ring to full effect with his footwork and speed, dancing and weaving around opponents throwing fast punches and then moving out of range.

His first recorded fight was against Harry Davis "The Coal Heaver" in 1780 at Mile End, London and after 40 minutes Harry Davis was severely punished. In the next three years Mendoza fought another twenty one opponents, winning the lot, perfecting his style along the way and although not all the fights were against top class fighters, it was all good experience for him. In March 1784 after an hour of fighting he beat the tough and durable Tom Tyne at Croydon, London, which reversed a defeat he suffered to Tyne in July of the previous year. In April 1787 at Barnet, London he fought big Sam Martin, a butcher and after eighteen rounds big Sam was laid out oblivious to the world. This upset a certain Richard Humphries who had fought Martin a year before, but it had taken him much longer to beat him. Humphries insulted Mendoza publicly, culminating in a challenge and the fight took place in January 1788 at Odiham, Hampshire. In a fiercely fought and even scrap Mendoza lost when he had to retire hurt after 28 minutes, his leg being trapped underneath him when Humphries fell on him. A return match was arranged for May the next year at Stilton, Cambridgeshire, where in the twenty second round Humphries is reputed to have gone down, without being hit, after a melee involving both sets of supporters. Order was restored and although Mendoza could have claimed victory for a foul, he decided to continue, eventually whipping Humphries in sixty five rounds. With one win each it was only natural that a decider was arranged for September 1790, with Mendoza again beating

Humphries in seventy two rounds taking 73 minutes in another epic contest at Doncaster, Yorkshire.

After Ben Brain retired in 1791, Mendoza laid claimed to the title once again as he had done when Tom Johnson temporarily retired in 1790, as Humphries had been regarded as the best fighter in England up until Mendoza had beaten him. Mendoza toured Ireland and beat the well-known Irish amateur Squire Fitzgerald, after the squire had insulted him. Bill Warr from Bristol also claimed the title, so the pair finally met at Croydon, London in 1792, where Mendoza won in twenty three rounds, to be declared the generally recognized champion, then Mendoza beat Warr again in 1794, in 15 minutes at Bexleyheath, Kent.

Over the years Mendoza, a poor businessman spent his money enjoying himself and picking up fights along the way to replenish his finances. In April 1795 at the age of 31 his prowess was in decline when he met "Gentleman" John Jackson for the championship at Hornchurch, Essex and Jackson battered Mendoza to defeat in just over 10 minutes. Mendoza retired and set up a boxing academy near the Strand, but again because of financial problems he returned to the ring in March 1806 when he beat Harry Lee and then again fourteen years later, when he lost to Tom Owen in 1820 at the age of 56 at Banstead Downs. He then kept a pub, the Admiral Nelson at Whitechapel, London where he and his wife raised 11 children. He died aged 72 in 1836 and his memoirs were the first to be written by a prize fighter.

1780-1782

Mendoza fought 22 opponents during these years winning all of them. They were Harry the Coalheaver, Tom Wilson, John Horn, Henry Davis, John Lloyd, Thomas Monk, John Hind, William Moore, John Williams, George Cannon, Al Fuller, Tom Spencer, John Knight, George McKenzie, William Taylor, John Baintree, George Hoast, John Hall, George Barry, William Cannon, Bill Move and George Smith.

1783

Tom Tyne, Leytonstone, London	L		75min.	10gns.
John Matthews, Kilburn Wells, London	W		120min.	12gns.
Richard Dennis, Lock Fields, London	W		30 min.	2gns.

1784

Tom Tyne, Croydon, London	W	27 r.	60min.	20gns.
William Bryan, Islington, London	D		30min.	

1785

William Nelson, London	W		75min.	40gns.

1787
Sam Martin, Barnet   W   18r.   31min.   25gns.

1788
Richard Humphries, Odiham, Hants.   L   28min.   300gns.
Mendoza was forced to retire through injury.

1789
Richard Humphries, Stilton, Cambs.   W   65r.   70min.   850gns.

1790
Claimed the Championship of England after Tom Johnson's retirement.
Richard Humphries, Doncaster, Yorks.   W   72r.   73min.   260gns.

1791
Squire Fitzgerald, Dublin (room-fight)   W   26min.   50gns.

1792
Bill Warr, Croydon, London   W   23r.   76min.   £500
Won the Championship of England.

1794
Bill Warr, Bexley Common, Kent   W   5r.   15min.   200gns.

1795
John Jackson, Hornchurch, Essex   L   9r.   11min.   400gns.
Lost the Championship.

1806
Harry Lee, Grimstead Green, near Bromley,
    Kent   W   53r.   67min.   50gns.

1820
Tom Owen, Banstead Downs, Surrey   L   12r.   15min.   50gns.

John Jackson
(Champion of England 1795-1796)

Born: 1769   Died: 1845

"Gentleman Jackson"

Born in London, John Jackson grew up to be an outstanding athlete as a sprinter and a long jumper, however much to his family's annoyance it was pugilism that attracted him most of all. Jackson stood 5' 11" and weighed about 196lbs. and was armed with a pleasant and polite disposition and armed with these attributes John Jackson decided to join the profession of prize fighting.

It took some time to find his first opponent but one was eventually found in the form of William Fewterell, a Birmingham giant weighing over 238 lbs. They met at Smitham Bottom, Croydon in June 1788. Slow and ponderous, Fewterell, who had won all his previous twenty fights proved no match for the speed, science and skills of Jackson and was thrashed soundly in just over an hour.

Almost a year later, in March 1789, Jackson took on George Inglestone, a brewer at Ingatestone, Essex and on a rain sodden day and a slippery stage ring, Jackson was winning the early stages of the fight and almost had the beating of his opponent, when he slipped in round five, breaking his leg and dislocating his ankle. Although Jackson begged to carry on, even apparently suggesting that the pair of them sat on stools and took lumps out of each other, it was just impossible and therefore he had to forfeit the fight and purse.

After some years of inactivity most people thought Jackson had retired, during which time, Daniel Mendoza had gained the English Championship; so friends of Jackson then urged him to challenge Mendoza for the title. Mendoza, although a popular champion was always in trouble with the law and it was thought that if a reputable man like John Jackson could win the title, then prize fighting would gain a better reputation. The match was made for April 1795 at Hornchurch, Essex, Mendoza being the favourite as Jackson had not fought for six years, while the champion had been regularly active. Jackson and Mendoza had both trained hard for the fight and although both men were very skilful boxers, it was Jackson with his physical advantage who wore Mendoza down and although there was some dispute over a so called foul blow by Jackson, the fight continued at such a frantic pace that it was all over in just 10 minutes and nine rounds of fighting, with Jackson the winner.

After this fight Jackson retired and bought a pub in Surrey that was visited by the gentry. He dressed in the latest fashions and became highly respected. He later opened a training academy and when the Pugilistic Club was founded in 1814 he was its most influential figure. Several years after he retired some of the boxing fraternity tried to drum up another fight between Jackson and Mendoza but John Jackson was having none of it, stating quite clearly that he had retired and was staying retired. He refereed the infamous bout between Simon Byrne and Sandy McKay in 1827 when Sandy McKay died as the result of his injuries, although Byrne was cleared of manslaughter.

John Jackson died of paralysis at his home in Grosvenor Street, London in October 1845, aged 76.

1788
William Fewterell, Smitham Bottom,
  Croydon   W   67min.

1789
George Ingleston, Ingatestone, Essex   L   5r.   20min.   50gns.

1795
Daniel Mendoza, Hornchurch, Essex   W   9r.   11min.   400gns.
Won the Championship of England.

Tom Owen
(Champion of England 1796-1797)

Born: 1768   Died: 1843

"The Fighting Oilman"

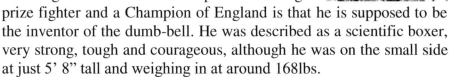

Tom Owen was born in Portsea near Portsmouth and his greatest claim to fame apart from being a prize fighter and a Champion of England is that he is supposed to be the inventor of the dumb-bell. He was described as a scientific boxer, very strong, tough and courageous, although he was on the small side at just 5' 8" tall and weighing in at around 168lbs.

His first recorded fight was against Bill Savage at Portsea near Portsmouth which he won in 60 minutes. He claimed the title after John Jackson's retirement from the ring by the sole reason of his defeat of William Hooper, "The Tinman" in fifty rounds at Harrow in November 1796. This claim of Owen's was not recognized in all quarters, Hooper was the favourite because he had previously been involved in some tough battles with the likes of big Ben Brain, Wright the Carpenter and a big strong man known only as Bunner. However, in the fight with Owen, Hooper dislocated his shoulder and so eventually lost to a man who was only rated as a mere beginner and novice.

Tom Owen then beat Hooper again in February 1797, but in August 1797 he lost his disputed claim on the championship to the highly rated Jack Bartholomew on Sunbury Common, Surrey in 30 minutes. In a well fought contest Tom Owen put up a strong challenge and Jack Bartholomew had to use all his experience and skill to finally overcome Owen. Tom Owen didn't fight again until September 1799 when he lost to a man named Housa the Jew in 42 minutes on Enfield Racecourse. He was so badly beaten he was carried to Enfield Hospital to recover, but was back later in the year to beat a man called Jack Davis, a local excavator, at Deptford in an hour of fighting. In 1800 he fought a man only known as "The Fighting Tar" at Portsmouth and won in 50 minutes, after which he retired from prizefighting.

Years later in 1804 when he was a second to Joe Berks in his fight with Henry Pearce "The Game Chicken" he stuffed a handkerchief into Berks mouth to stop him crying out his submission! Owen was jailed for three months after this fight and charged with helping to cause a riot and conspiracy. He came out of retirement and beat Daniel Mendoza in 12 rounds at Banstead Downs, Surrey, however this was in 1820 when Owens was 52 and Mendoza 56! He later owned a pub, The Shipwrights Arms in Northfleet, Kent where he probably gave the customers the odd song, because he was reputed to be quite a good singer. He died in 1843 at the age of 74.

Undated

Bill Savage, Portsea, Hants.	W		60min.	

1796

William Hooper, Harrow, Middx.	W	50r.	64min.	200gns.

Claimed as for the Championship of England.

1797

William Hooper, near Harrow, Middx.	W			100gns.

Retained the Championship.

Jack Bartholomew, Moulsey Hurst, Surrey	L	26r.	30min.	50gns.

Lost the Championship.

1799

Housa the Jew. Enfield, London	L		42min.	10gns.
Jack Davis, Deptford, London	W		60min.	

1800

The Fighting Tar, Portsmouth, Hants.	W		50min.	20gns.

1820

Daniel Mendoza, Banstead Downs, Surrey	W	12r.	15min.	50gns.

Jack Bartholomew
(Champion of England 1797-1800)

Born: 1763   Died: 1803

"Barty"

The son of a London gardener from Brentford, Jack Bartholomew was reputed to be a skilful, brave and hard hitting fighter. He was 5' 10" tall and weighed about 168lbs. throughout his ring career. His first known fight was a hard fought win in 50 minutes against Jack Fearby, a man known as "The Young Ruffian", on Hounslow Heath in June 1795. He then fought and lost on a foul to William Wood in January 1797 and then in August of the same year on Sunbury Common, outside London he beat unofficially recognized champion Tom Owen in an epic contest in 30 minutes. Although some historians do not accept this as a championship fight it has to be remembered that it appears there was no one else stepping forward to challenge these two fighters, so Jack Bartholomew gained justifiable recognition for his skills and victory, by being recognized as Champion of England. This accolade was further enhanced when in January 1800 at St. George's Field on the Uxbridge Road, just outside London he fought the brilliant and up and coming young star, Jem Belcher to a draw over fifty one rounds with both men unable to carry on through exhaustion and on the point of collapse.

At this period in his life Bartholomew was employed by the very eccentric Lord Camelford as a personal bodyguard and eminent sponsor and backed him to the tune of 300 guineas when Jack again took on Jem Belcher at Finchley Common in May 1800. Belcher eventually overcame Bartholomew, although it was an extremely close and tough fight. By the third round Belcher was so badly beaten that a black pigeon was released to signal his defeat to his friends at home, however he somehow made it up to the scratch for the fourth round, rallied because Bartholomew could not find the killer punch to finish him and finally Belcher saw off the brave Bartholomew in round seventeen, when he caught Jack with a terrific left, Bartholomew's head hitting the ground with a thud, leaving him unable to defend himself. On top of this, after the fight, Jack Bartholomew was arrested for a breach of the peace!

He died in 1803, officially from cirrhosis of the liver, but many believe it was the terrible punishment that he took in his prizefighting career and although only five of his fights are recorded, he, like numerous others probably had many more.

1795
Jack Firby, Hounslow, Middx.   W   13r.   50min.   10gns.

1797
Will Wood, Ealing near Harrow   LF   15r.   16min.   100gns.
Tom Owen, Sunbury Common, London   W   26r.   30min.   50gns.
Recognized as for the Championship of England.

1800
Jem Belcher, St George's Field, London   D   51r.   40min.   40gns.
Retained the Championship.
Jem Belcher,Finchley Common, London   L   17r.   20min.   300gns.
Lost the Championship.

Jem Belcher
(Champion of England 1800-1805)

Born: 1781   Died: 1811

"Napoleon of the Ring"

Born in Bristol in 1781, Jem Belcher became one of the all-time great bare knuckle prize fighters, with quite a pedigree in the sport, as his grandfather was Jack Slack who held the championship some 50 years before. He stood just less than 6' 0" tall and weighed just under 154lbs. at the start of his career and up to 175lbs. later on.

As a teenager he trained for some time in the butchery trade and after fighting some seasoned fighters at the local Lansdowne Fair, at Bath, Jem Belcher fought his first professional bout in his home town in 1798. He defeated Jack (Bob) Britton, a pugilist of some repute who later fought the great Dutch Sam, but against Belcher Jack Britton was battered to defeat after 30 minutes and Belcher then went on to defeat Jem Lockley, who was beaten in 25 minutes.

Belcher moved to London, under the supervision of ex-fighter Bill Warr and in April 1799 he trounced the experienced "Paddington" Jones in sixteen rounds, then he fought the highly rated Jack Bartholomew to a fifty one round draw in January 1800. At the time, Bartholomew was considered the Champion of England, or the nearest thing to it by some quarters because he had beaten another highly rated title-claimant, Tom Owen. When Belcher soundly beat Bartholomew after seventeen rounds, in a return fight in May 1800 at Finchley Common, London he was hailed as the new champion by the majority of the fighting world and he was still not 20 years of age!

He went on to knock out George Baker "The Norfolk Gypsy" and then the Irish champion, Andrew Gamble on Wimbledon Common in five rounds in front of a very large crowd. In 1801 he beat Joe Berks three times, in July on Wimbledon Common, then in November in sixteen rounds at Hurley Bottom near Maidenhead, Berkshire and then yet again in August 1802 near Hyde Park, London in thirteen rounds. After that Belcher disposed of Jack Fearby "The Young Ruffian", who was severely punished in eleven rounds in April 1803 near Newmarket, Suffolk.

Tragedy then struck in July of that year when Belcher was blinded in his right eye by the ball in a game of racquets. Half blind, he did not defend his title for two years, fighting exhibition bouts only and running The Two Brewers pub in London. In the meantime Jem Belcher's friend, Henry Pearce "The Game Chicken" made a claim to the championship because of Belcher's retirement, so the not so fit Belcher agreed to a title fight with Pearce and they met at Blythe, Nottinghamshire in December 1805. Hindered by the loss of the eye and his publican lifestyle, the talk was also that Belcher needed the money. Not really fit enough to take the rigours of a brutal prize fight, especially against the likes of Pearce, Belcher could not stand up to the aggressive "Chicken" and a game and plucky Jem Belcher had to eventually submit after hard fought fight after eighteen rounds and therefore relinquishing his title of Champion of England.

In April 1807 Belcher agreed to fight the highly rated Tom Cribb and the fight attracted a large crowd to Mousley Hurst, Surrey as Jem Belcher was still a great favourite of the Fancy. For the first twenty rounds, again the brave and gallant Belcher treated the spectators to a master class of boxing, but then Cribb hit Belcher over his good eye, nearly closing it. Cribb was even knocked down after eighteen rounds and had also broken his hand, but the fight was allowed to continue and shrugging off the pain from his broken hand Cribb began to dominate. Belcher's hands were also seriously injured and finally, after forty one rounds, the heroic and brave Jem Belcher was forced to concede the fight. In February 1809 in a rematch on Epsom Downs, Surrey, Cribb again eventually outclassed and quelled the artistry and courage of Belcher and won in thirty one rounds. Ruined financially by this fight Jem Belcher served four weeks in prison for starting a fracas after the fight and while in there he became seriously ill. Having recovered, although never a completely well man after this, he ran the Coach & Horses pub in Soho, London.

Illness struck the unlucky Jem Belcher once again, finally taking the life of one of the most skillful and gamest prize fighters ever to enter the prize ring, when he died in 1811 and was buried in St. Anne's Churchyard, Soho, London aged just 30 years old. One wonders how many more wins he could have won but for the loss of his eye.

1793
At the age of 12, although no other facts are known, Belcher beat the Cockroader, a Corporal, Norton and Pawlett, all at the local Lansdowne Fair near Bath.

1798

Bob Britton, Bristol	W		33min.	20gns.
Jem Lockley, Lansdowne Fair, Bristol	W		25min.	

1799

Paddington Jones, Wormwood Scrubs, London	W	16r.	33min.	50gns.

1800

Jack Batholomew, St. George's Fields, off Uxbridge Road, London	D	51r.	40min.	40gns.
For the Championship of England.				
Jack Bartholomew, Finchley Common, London	W	17r.	20min.	300gns.
Won the Championship of England.				
George Baker, *unknown venue*	WKO			
Andrew Gamble, Wimbledon Common, London	W	5r.	10min.	100gns.

1801

Joe Berks, Wimbledon Common, London (turn-up)	W		19min.	
Joe Berks, Hurley Bottom, Berks.	W	16r.		100gns.
Retained the Championship.				

1802

Joe Berks, Hyde Park, London	W	13r.	10min.	250gns.
Retained the Championship.				

1803

Jack Firby, Linton, Cambs.	W	11r.	20min.	100gns.
Retained the Championship.				

1805

Hen Pearce, Blythe, Notts.	L	18r.	35min.	500gns.
Lost the Championship.				

1807

Tom Cribb, Moulsey Hurst, Surrey	L	41r.	55min.	£400
For the Championship of England.				

1809

Tom Cribb, Epsom Downs, Surrey	L	31r.	40min.	200gns.
For the Championship of England.				

Henry "Hen" Pearce
(Champion of England 1805-1807)

Born: 1777   Died: 1809

"The Game Chicken"

Born in Bristol in 1777 Henry Pearce served an apprenticeship until the age of 21, but he started fighting as a boy in fights arranged by his father. Standing only 5' 9" and weighing about 168lbs.-182lbs. throughout his ring career, he was by no means a big man but became one of the unbeaten greats with his fast, hard hitting style.

He arrived in London around 1803 and easily beat Jack Fearby, "The Young Ruffian", in a ten foot square ring in the back room of a pub. Pearce was nominated by his fellow Bristolian, Jem Belcher, who had retired through his eye injury, as his successor to the title, but Joe Berks immediately challenged this move, not only because he thought he was the rightful contender, if not the rightful champion, but because of his genuine grudge of Pearce, a close friend of Belcher, who he also held a grudge against. When they eventually met in the prize ring Pearce twice smashed Joe Berks to defeat, firstly in August 1803 in fifteen rounds and then in January 1804 in twenty four rounds to be generally recognized as the rightful champion by the Fancy and the sporting press.

He then went on to defeat a formidable Elias Spree near Hampton Court, London in March 1805 in twenty nine rounds and then immediately after the fight he accepted the challenge of the giant 6' 3" Tom Carte of Birmingham, beating the Birmingham man in twenty five rounds in a very one-sided fight the next month of the same year at Shepperton Common, London.

In 1805, he fought a memorable and strange battle with his friend John Gully, a fellow West Country man and an inmate of the debtors' prison. The fight was arranged to get Gully out of prison by making out Gully was a prize fighter and deserved to be out of prison and training to be a top class pugilist (a feat he later attained). The two met in a "set up" fight in the prison grounds with Gully getting the best of Pearce by a small margin. Ideally impressed with his opponent's showing, Pearce arranged for a sponsor called Fletcher Reid to pay Gully's debts so that he could be released from prison. The two then met for real at Hailsham, Sussex in October 1805 and in a classic contest Pearce beat Gully in sixty four rounds. Pearce dominated Gully early in the fight, knocking him down in each of the first seven rounds. In the eighteenth round, Gully came back to batter Pearce. In the twentieth round, one of Pearce's eyes was so swollen that it was nearly fully closed. However, from round thirty three until the end of the fight, Pearce was in control and after 77 minutes his persistent attack sufficiently weakened Gully to such an extent that he could not continue.

Pearce laid full claim to the title in his next fight, when he faced his old friend Jem Belcher, who had never lost his title in the ring, when Jem was persuaded out of retirement. Pearce outfought the brave one eyed Belcher for eighteen rounds to win the undisputed championship at Blythe, Nottinghamshire in December 1805. From here it was all downhill for Hen Pearce because he never fought in the prize ring again. He was to have fought Gully in a return in 1807 but his health was now declining and his marriage was by now over. Women and gin led to a rapid decline in his health and by 1807 he was drifting from town to town, giving exhibition fights for a few pounds and reminiscing back on his past glories to anyone who would listen, to earn a bob or two.

After returning to his home town of Bristol with a new wife he seemed to settle down for a little while and was temporarily sober when giving a good hiding to three gamekeepers on Clifton Downs for insulting a woman. He also turned out to be a hero in November 1807 when he came to the rescue of a 17 year old girl, when saving her from a drapery shop fire in the city. However by 1808 he had contracted tuberculosis and in April 1809 when a benefit was held for him he only barely made it, dying less than three weeks later. He was 32 years old.

1803

Jack Firby, Bond Street, London (room fight)	W	10r.	30min.
Joe Berks, London	W	15r.	20min.	350

Claimed the Championship of England as Belcher had retired.

1804

Joe Berks, Putney Green, London	W	24r.	77min.	£100+purse

Generally recognized as for the Championship of England.

51

1805

Elias Spray, Moulsey Hurst, Surrey	W	29r.	35min.	100gns.
Retained the Championship.				
Tom Carte, Shepperton Common, Surrey	W	25r.	35min.	100gns.
Retained the Championship.				
John Gully, Hailsham, Sussex	W	64r.	77min.	600gns.
Retained the Championship.				
Jem Belcher, Blythe, Notts.	W	18r.	35min.	1000gns.
Retained the Championship.				

John Gully
(Champion of England 1807-1808)

Born: 1783   Died: 1863

"The Potter"

John Gully was born at the Rose & Crown
pub, at Wick near Bristol, the son of a butcher.
Legend has it that he sent the eighteen stone
local bruiser "Sixteen String" Jack Rand,
unconscious and home in a cart after accepting his challenge at the
local Lansdowne Fair. This was reputed to have taken place in
September 1803 making Gully about twenty at the time. He had all
the attributes of a first class pugilist as he was a fast, strong and
scientific boxer, 6' 0" tall and weighing in at around 189lbs.

Gully took over the family business when his father died but by
1804 and lacking the business acumen of his father, he had run the
business down and into serious debt. He decided to leave the business
and the city of Bristol rather quickly and was chased all the way to
London before his creditors finally caught up with him. Gully was
sentenced and jailed, but was only there for about a year before being
rescued by his friend and fellow Bristolian, the pugilist, Hen Pearce.
Pearce had found a sponsor to pay Gully's debt through an
arrangement for Gully to fight Pearce in a rather dubious fight in the
confines of the jail. Gully is supposed to have won this "fixed" fight
and the jail authorities, impressed by Gulley's performance against
Pearce apparently let him be released on the condition that when he
was freed he would become a prize fighter.

Out of jail Gully kept his promise and was taken to a training camp
in Egham, Surrey where he was trained up to full fitness, to then
challenge his friend Hen Pearce for the Championship of England,
which had been allegedly engineered for Gully to win by Pearce's
backers after Hen Pearce retired. Knowing they were friends, the
boxing fraternity smelt a rat, so when the two men and their seconds
met on the field of combat in May 1805, the crowd turned ugly,
forcing Gully and Pearce to do a runner. However after eventually
impressing people with his prowess in the gym against several
roughnecks and a warm up fight against a corporal guardsman, which

Gully won in August 1805, a fight between Pearce and Gully was resurrected and the two met in October of that same year at Hailsham, Sussex. In a tremendous and bloody contest both men gave and received no quarter, although by round twenty Gully was getting the better of Pearce. Pearce though would not give in and after continuously being pummelled around the ring, he found the strength to knock Gully clean off his feet in round sixty four and so retain his title. A return was arranged for September 1807 but Hen Pearce had to retire through ill health and so relinquished the championship.

A title fight was then arranged in October 1807 at Newmarket, Suffolk for Gully to meet the giant Bob Gregson, who Gully then proceeded to destroy in thirty six rounds after 80 minutes of fighting and then again in May 1808 at Woburn, Bedfordshire, Gully again beat him in twenty eight rounds, earning the right to the title and although it is said that he declined the honour, he was still recognized as the Champion of England. After the second Gregson fight Gully decided to retire and could not be enticed back into the ring again. After running a pub he became interested in horse racing and eventually became a millionaire, a Member of Parliament and a successful race horse owner. He died in 1863 at the age 79, a very rich man although once a convict and a pauper!

1803

Jack Rand, Lansdowne Fair, Bath	W			

1805

Hen Pearce, Debtor's Prison, London (gloves)	EX	5r.		
A Corporal Guardsman, London	W			
Hen Pearce, Hailsham, Surrey	L	64r.	77min.	600gns.

For the Championship of England.

1807

Bob Gregson,, Six Mile Bottom, Newmarket, Suffolk	W	36r.	80min.	200gns.

Won the Championship of England.

1808

Bob Gregson, Woburn, Beds.	W	28r.	75min.	200gns.

Retained the Championship.

Tom Cribb
(Champion of England 1808-1822)

Born: 1781   Died: 1848

"The Black Diamond"

Tom Cribb is another prize fighter rated in history as one of the great bare knuckle champions and although some critics at the time described his style as ungainly, even cumbersome and crude, no one doubted his courage, durability and strength. At 5' 11" in height he had a fighting weight of just over 196lbs. and was another top fighter who hailed from the West Country city of Bristol. Born in 1781, by the time he was 13 he had, like others before him, made his way to London where he worked on the docks and wharfs.

His first recorded fight was against the tough and durable George Maddox in January 1805, in which he struggled to beat the fifty year old veteran, eventually overcoming him in seventy six arduous rounds. In the same year he also collected wins against Tom Blake and Ikey Pig, but this winning streak came to a halt when he surprisingly lost to George Nicholls; however he ended 1805 with a win over Bill Richmond known as the "The Black Terror".

When Jem Belcher retired as champion in 1803, Hen Pearce claimed the title, so Belcher came out of retirement only to bravely lose to Pearce. Belcher was then matched with Cribb, the fight taking place at Moulsey Hurst, Surrey in April 1807, where Cribb, in an epic fight, defeated Belcher in forty one rounds. In May 1808 Cribb defeated George Horton at Woburn, Buckinghamshire in twenty five rounds and was then victorious in a punishing fight with Bob Gregson at Moulsey Hurst, Surrey in the October of that same year which took twenty three rounds, with Cribb claiming the Championship of England.

Jem Belcher again tried to regain the title when he and Cribb faced each other for a second time at Epsom Downs, Surrey in February 1809. The fight lasted thirty one rounds with Belcher winning the early rounds, but with only one eye, he finally and bravely succumbed to the more powerful Cribb who was then truly recognized as Champion of England by the Fancy.

Tom Cribb then announced his retirement but Tom Molyneaux, an American by birth, immediately challenged Cribb for his title, so Cribb came out of retirement and at Copthall Common, Sussex in December 1810 they faced each other. Molyneaux took the fight to the champion and in round twenty eight, after he had almost knocked out Cribb, it was suggested by Cribb's second that Molyneaux was carrying weights in his hands. It was untrue, but the time wasted checking this claim gave Cribb sufficient time to recover and he then proceeded to defeat Molyneaux after twelve more rounds. It has often been suggested that because no one wanted an American by birth to covet the Championship of England, Cribb's seconds came up with this time wasting ruse, or what would be called gamesmanship today, and it worked, because Molyneaux would probably have won if it was not for this ruse by Cribb's corner.

Cribb retired once again, Molyneaux challenged him once again and Cribb came out of retirement once again with the two pugilists facing each other this time at Thistleton Gap, Rutland in September 1811. Again Molyneaux started stronger but Cribb tossed him heavily in the seventh round, battering Molyneaux to defeat by round eleven. It must be remembered that in the first fight between the pair, the title came its closest so far to being won for the first time by someone not from these shores and many felt that Molyneaux was robbed of the title, simply because it was unthinkable that the English championship title could be won by someone not from England and especially by a black man, whose ethnic origin at the time was considered inferior.

Tom Cribb fought mainly exhibition matches and giving after dinner speeches at boxing dinners after that, until he officially retired in 1822. He was the well-respected landlord of the Union Arms public house in Piccadilly, London for many years and died after a lingering illness at the age of 67.

1805

George Maddox, Wood Green, London	W	76r.	13min.	25gns.
Tom Blake, Blackheath, London	W	20r.	69min.	40gns.
Ikey Pig, Blackheath, London	W	11r.	35min.	50gns.
George Nichols, Blackwater, Hants.	LF	52r.	90min.	£25
Bill Richmond, Hailsham, Sussex	W	24r.	90min.	25gns.

1807

Jem Belcher, Moulsey Hurst, Surrey	W	41r.	55mins	£400

Claimed the Championship of England.

1808

George Horton,, near Market Street, Woburn, Herts.	W	25r		100gns.

Claimed as for the Championship of England

Bob Gregson, Moulsey Hurst, Surrey	W	23r.	45min.	500gns.

Won the Championship of England.

1809

Jem Belcher, Epsom Downs, Surrey	W	31r.	40min.	200gns.

Retained the Championship.

1810

Tom Molineaux, Copthall Common, Sussex	W	44r.	55min.	50gns.

Retained the Championship.

1811

Tom Molineaux, Thisleton Gap, Rutland	W	11r.	20min	£600

Retained the Championship.

1812-1816

Turn ups recorded in London against Symonds the Jew, Massa Kendrick and an unknown soldier with Cribb winning them all.

1820

Jack Carter, London (room-fight)	W	1r.	1min.

Tom Spring
(Champion of England 1823-1824)

Born: 1795   Died: 1851

"The Light Tapper"

Tom Spring was born near Hereford in 1795. Where the surname Spring came from is a mystery as his real surname was Winter (something to do with the seasons perhaps). He was an apprentice to a butcher but also took up boxing and was described as a clever, neat and courageous boxer, although he didn't carry a particularly powerful punch, hence his nickname "The Light Tapper". Spring was a well-built man who stood just under 6' 0" tall and weighed around 189lbs.

His career started with wins over John Hollands and Jack Henley in rounds fifteen and eleven respectively, at Mordiford, Herefordshire in 1812 and 1814 respectively. His next fight is recorded as in September 1817, when he beat Jack Stringer at Moulsey Hurst, Surrey in twenty nine rounds, then thrashed Ned Painter in thirty one rounds at Mickleham Downs, near Leatherhead, Surrey in April 1818. In a return, four months later, at Kingston-upon-Thames, Ned Painter reversed the result beating Spring in forty two rounds. In May 1819, Spring took on highly rated Jack Carter at Crawley Downs, Surrey and defeated him in a tough seventy one round contest. After that, in May 1820 he beat Bob Burn at Epsom Downs, Surrey in eighteen rounds, Josh Hudson in five rounds and Tom Oliver followed in February 1821 being beaten by Spring in twenty five rounds. Then Tom Spring advertised in the newspapers that he was willing to take on anyone in the land and when Tom Cribb, the recognized champion retired in 1822 he nominated Tom Spring as his successor and as the English champion. Bill Neat, who also considered himself champion, stepped forward in May 1823 and faced Spring at Andover for the title, but unfortunately for Neat he broke his arm in round four, which stopped him from continuing after another four rounds, with Spring being declared as the new undisputed champion.

In 1824 Tom Spring fought Jack Langan, the new Irish star in what was to be two of the classic title prize fights of the time. First, in

January at Worcester Racecourse where in a fight that started with Spring having the best of it, then Langan taking the middle stages and then Spring coming back as Langan faded; it ended in round seventy seven with Langan out cold. The return near Warwick in June of the same year, followed much the same pattern as the first fight, with Spring the more sprightly at the start, however by the middle stages Langan was exhausted and Spring had badly damaged hands. Spring couldn't hit Langan hard because of the state of his hands, however Langan held on until round seventy six, when he finally collapsed with exhaustion, after what was no more than a slap from Spring.

Tom Spring retired after this fight to run the Castle Tavern in Holborn until his death in 1851 aged 56.

1812
John Hollands, Mordiford, Herefordshire	W	15r.	45min.	

1814
Jack Henley, Mordiford, Herefordshire	W	11r.		6gns.

1817
Jack Stringer, Moulsey Hurst, Surrey	W	29r.	39min.	10gns.

1818
Ned Painter, Micklesham Downs, Surrey	W	31r.	89min.	200gns.
Ned Painter, Russia Farm, Kingston-upon-Thames London	L	42r.	64min.	100gns

1819
Jack Carter, Crawley Downs, Sussex	W	71r.	115min.	£150
Ben Burn, Wimbledon, London	W	11r.	18min.	£40

1820
Young Bob Burn, Epsom Downs, Surrey	W	18r.	30min.	£200
Josh Hudson, Moulsey Hurst, Surrey	W	5r.	10min.	£20

1821
Tom Oliver, Arlington Corner, Hayes, Middx.	W	25r.	55min.	200gns.

1823
Bill Neat, Andover, Hants	W	8r.	37min.	£400

Won the Championship of England.

1824
Jack Langan, Worcester	W	77r.	149min.	£600

Retained the Championship.

Jack Langan, Birdham Bridge, near Chichester, Sussex	W	76r.	109min.	£1,000

Retained the Championship.

Tom Cannon
(Champion of England 1824-1825)

Born: 1790   Died: 1858

"The Great Gun of Windsor"

Tom Cannon was born near Windsor, at Eton, Berkshire in 1790 and was considered an all-round sportsman, especially at cricket and rowing, earning his money as a waterman and fisherman; it was in 1814 through fishing, that he was unlucky to be caught in the wrong place at the wrong time and fined, but moved rather quickly and conveniently to Newbury in the west of the county of Berkshire without paying! Before that though he had a few minor fights which went unrecorded, apart from one in 1809 against Tom Anslow at the Slough Fair which Cannon won in 30 minutes. Not until 1817 is another fight recorded, when he won in sixty rounds over Bill "Dolly" Smith at Maidenhead, Berkshire which apparently started out as a dispute over a raffle. Tom Cannon was about 5' 10" in height, weighing between 168lbs.-182lbs. and known as a strong, durable fighter with a good punch.

There is no recorded evidence of Cannon fighting again until June 1824, when he, in what was thought audacious by the Fancy, challenged Josh Hudson, a seasoned professional who had been in with Jem Ward only a year earlier; however Cannon outclassed an overweight and unfit Hudson at Blackwater, Hampshire in seventeen rounds and in doing so claimed the championship title, which immediately provoked a challenge for a return contest from Hudson. This was accepted and in November of that same year at Stanfield Park, Warwickshire a much fitter and leaner Hudson was again defeated this time in sixteen rounds and with this win Tom Cannon again claimed the vacant championship title. This claim was again disputed in a challenge by Jem Ward, so in July 1825 the two met at Warwick and in a brutal 10 minutes of fighting, Cannon lost his claim to the title when he was knocked out by Ward, who was then generally recognized by the Fancy as the new champion. Tom Cannon only fought once more, when he was beaten by Ned Neale in February 1827, in twenty two rounds at Warfield, Berkshire.

Tom Cannon retired after this fight and ran The Castle pub in Jermyn Street, London. When that eventually failed, his health gradually failed as well, depression set in and in July 1858 he committed suicide. He was 68 years old.

1809

Tom Anslow, Slough Fair, Berks.	W		32min.	6gns.

1817

Dolly Smith, Maidenhead, Berks	W	60r.	64min.	20gns.

1824

Josh Hudson, Blackwater, Hants.	W	17r.	21min.	£100
Claimed the Championship of England.				
Josh Hudson, Warwick	W	16r.	20min.	£1,000
Won the Championship of England.				

1825

Jem Ward, Warwick	L	10r.	10min.	£1,000
Lost the Championship.				

1827

Ned Neale, Warfield, Berks.	L	22r.	30min.	£200

Jem Ward
(Champion of England 1825-1832)

Born: 1800   Died: 1884

"The Black Diamond"

Born in London in 1800, Jem Ward at 5' 10" and weighing around 175lbs. possessed brilliant skills as a boxer, painter and musician, but it was boxing that he is known for best. He worked as a coal whipper, a heavy manual job hauling loads of coal about in baskets. He took part and passed a professional boxing trial and his first recognized fights being when he defeated George Robinson in May 1816 and then followed this with another win against Bill Wall the next month. In July 1817 Jem Ward went on to defeat George Webb and then in 1819, Jack Murray and Nick Murphy in February and July respectively.

The year of 1820 saw Ward defeat Mike Hayes in September and Jack Delaney in October, all of Ward's fight being held around the London area and these wins soon brought him to the attention of the Fancy and the London Prize Ring, although in his next contest against Dick Acton his win in six rounds in June 1822 was just outside London at Moulsey Hurst, Surrey. After another win against Jack Burke at Harpenden, Hertfordshire this mercurial start was then tainted when he "threw" his next fight, also in 1822, against Bill Abbott, after he alleged he was threatened with serious injury from the Abbott camp if he had won. He was expelled by the Pugilistic Society but Ward was reinstated the next year, subsequently losing to Josh Hudson in November 1823. He picked himself up from this defeat to then go on and defeat Phil Sampson twice in June and October 1824, in twenty five and twenty seven rounds respectively.

Tom Cannon's claim as titleholder was disputed by Jem Ward, so in July 1825 at Warwick they met in a brutal contest that only lasted 10 minutes with Ward taking the title from Cannon. Ward then went on a sparring tour, claiming that any would be contenders would have to fight it out amongst themselves to find the next worthy challenger. The outcome was a title fight with Peter Crawley in January 1827 at Royston, Hertfordshire in which, at the start, Ward was winning, but by round nine Crawley had got himself back into the fight. Although both boxers were near to exhaustion, Crawley found the strength in round eleven to knock Ward out cold with a stunning left to the head. Crawley immediately retired, so Ward refused to hand over the title belt, reclaimed the title and sent a challenge forthwith to anyone who thought they were worthy to fight him for it. No one immediately stepped forward, so in 1828 the Fancy pitched into the limelight a thirty eight year old ex-convict who had done a bit of boxing, a certain Jack Carter and in May, at Shepperton, Surrey that same year, Jack Carter managed to last seventeen rounds until his seconds threw in the sponge. Jem Ward fought for the last time against Simon Byrne in July 1831, near Stratford-on-Avon and outclassed Byrne, who put up little fight, beating him in thirty three rounds.

Upon retirement Jem Ward toured America, although there is no record of any fights there and lived to the grand old age of 83 until his death in 1884, making him one of the longest living known pugilists.

1816

George Robinson, Stepney, London	W		45min.	£20
Bill Wall, Limehouse, London	W		120min.	£20

1817

George Webb, Limehouse, London	W	1r.	3min.	£30

1819

Jack Murray, Dockhill, Shadwell, London	W		45min.	£30
Nick Murphy, Barking, Essex	W		35min.	£20

1820

Mike Hayes, Isle of Dogs, London	W		40min.	£30
John Delaney, Bow Common, London	W		30min.	£30

1822

Dick Acton, Moulsey Hurst, Surrey	W	6r.	15min.	£50+purse
Jack Burke, Harpenden, Herts	W	7r.	7min.	£2+purse
Bill Abbott, Moulsey Hurst, Surrey (fixed fight?)	L	22r.		£50

1823

Ned Baldwin, Wimbledon	W	20r.	19min.	£5+purse
Joe Rickens, Lansdowne, Bath	W	8r.	15min.	£40+purse
Jem Johnson, Southampton, Hants.	W	8r	18min.	purse
Josh Hudson, Moulsey Hurst, Surrey (fixed fight?)	L	15r.	36min.	200gns.

1824

Phil Sampson, Colnbrook, Bucks.	W	25r.	50min.	£200
Phil Sampson, Stony Stratford, Bucks.	W	27r.	37min.	£200

1825

Tom Cannon, Warwick	W	10r.	10min.	£1,000

Won the Championship of England

.

1826

Phil Sampson, Norwich (turn up-gloves)	W	10r.

1827

Peter Crawley, Royston, Herts.	L	11r.	26min.	£200

Lost the Championship but reclaimed it two days later because Crawley abdicated.

1828

Jack Carter, Shepperton Range, Surrey	W	17r.	32min.	£100

Retained the Championship.

1831

Simon Byrne, Willeycutt, Surrey	W	33r.	77min.	£400

Retained the Championship.

Peter Crawley
(Champion of England 1827)

Born: 1799   Died: 1865

"Young Rump Steak"

Born in Newington Green, London in 1799, Peter Crawley got the nickname "The Young Rump Steak" working as a butcher's boy. He grew into a 6' 0" feet muscular man who weighed around 182lbs. in his prime and was reputed to be a skilful, strong and durable fighter.

His first recorded fight, a turn up, was in 1815 against Pat Flannigan at Whitecross Street, London and resulted in victory for Crawley after only 15 minutes. In 1816 and 1817 he fought a total of ten known fights and turn ups, mostly in the London area, all resulting in wins before he was matched against Tom Watson in February 1818 at Gough Square, London and after two and a half hours the glove fight was declared a draw. Crawley then took on Ben Sutcliffe in his first recorded paid fight in August 1818 at Rushey Farm, Kingston, winning in seven rounds and then March 1819 saw him defeated for the only known time in his career when he lost in 14 minutes to the experienced Tom Hickman "The Gasman", at Moulsey Hurst, Surrey. He then went on in May 1822 to batter to defeat a man known only as "Southern's Bully", at Chester Racecourse during the Chester Fair and then proceeded to beat Dick Acton at Blindlow Heath in May of 1823. He also fought a few other fighters in the same year, whether they were genuine prize fights or turn ups there is now no trace.

Crawley now wanted to fight Jem Ward for the Championship of England but couldn't find a backer to put up the purse money until 1826 and so in early January 1827 the two met at Royston, Hertfordshire to fight for the title. Ward started well and threw Crawley in round seven, but the challenger began to continuously use his powerful left jab into Ward's body and face until another powerful left rendered Ward unconscious in round eleven, so introducing Peter Crawley as the new Champion of England. Two days later Peter Crawley announced his retirement from the ring and because of this the loser Jem Ward refused to hand over the championship belt, stating that he would never give it up to anyone who was not active in the ring. Crawley refused to meet Ward in the ring again and in fact Peter Crawley never did fight in the ring again, so Jem Ward reclaimed the title and looked around for a suitable challenger, which presented itself in the form of Jack Carter. After he retired Peter Crawley ran a pub and taught boxing, dying at 66 in 1865.

1815

Pat Flanagan, Whitecross Street, London	W		15min.	

1816-1817

Bill Hunt, Long Fields, London (turn-up)	W	3r.	10min.	
Jack Bennett, Clara Market, London	D		15min.	
Tom Price, Clara Market, London	W		20min.	
Bill Coleman	D			
Clare Market John	W	19r.		
Harry Buckstone (turn-up)	W			
Tim McCarthy, Long Fields, London	W		20min.	
Tom Tyler, Kent Road, London (turn-up)	W	1r.	1min.	
Shirley's Carman, Warwick Lane (turn-up)	W		30min.	
Big Drayman, Whitecross Street, London	W	4r.		

1818

Tom Watson, Gough Square, London	ND		150min.	
Ben Sutcliffe, Rushey Farm, Kingston-upon-Thames	W	7r.	10min.	£40

1819

Tom Hickman, Moulsey Hurst, Surrey	L	13r.	14min.	£100

1822

Southern's Bully, Chester Races (gloves)	W		50min.	

1823

Dick Acton, Blindlow Heath?	W	13r.	16min.	£100

1824

Won several minor fights.

1826

Unknown Engineer, London (private fight)	W			

1827

Jem Ward, Royston Heath, Herts.	W	11r.	26min.	£100

Won the Championship of England and retired two days later.

James Burke
(Champion of England 1833-1839)

Born: 1809   Died: 1845

"The Deaf 'Un"

James Burke was born in St. Giles, London in 1809, the son of Irish parents and although deaf and illiterate he grew up to be a reputed honest, courageous and scientific fighter who possessed a terrific punch in either hand, although he only stood 5' 8½" and weighed between 175lbs.-178lbs.

His first recorded fight at 18 years old was in February 1828, at Whetstone Common, Leicestershire, against Ned Murphy and after fifty rounds it was declared a draw when darkness fell. Burke fought three more times that year against George Murray, Thomas Hands and Young Sambo, winning all three. He started 1829 with wins against Young Berridge and Bill Fitzmaurice before his first defeat at the hands of Bill Couzens in one hundred and eleven rounds at Whetstone Common, Leicestershire and then finished off the year with another win in seventeen rounds against Jem Girdler at Northchapel, Sussex, in December.

The year 1830 brought wins against Andrew Gow, Bob Hampson and Tim Crawley and in the year of 1831, wins against Jack Davis and James Blissett. In May 1832 he defeated Jack Carter over eleven rounds at Woolwich, London and after this win, James Burke challenged Jem Ward for the title, but Ward declined and retired, so Burke claimed the title, which Harry Macone disputed. James Burke and Harry Macone met for the vacant title in January 1833 at Lockington, Yorkshire and Macone was defeated by the pounding fists of Burke after fifty nine rounds.

The next challenger to step forward was Simon Byrne and they clashed at No Man's Land, London in May 1833, in what was a brutal fight, with both fighters taking terrible punishment. After ninety nine rounds and Burke teetering on the edge of defeat, Byrne collapsed, with Burke declared the winner. Three days later Simon Byrne died of his injuries, Burke was arrested, was judged and then cleared for Byrne's death.

After an exhibition tour Burke travelled to America, where, in New Orléans in May 1837 he fought his arch rival Sam O'Rourke; however O'Rourke's gang of thugs broke the ring after three rounds and Burke had to flee for his life, the fight being judged as a no decision contest. He then fought and won against Tom O'Connell in New York in ten rounds in August of 1837.

On his arrival back in England James Burke was immediately challenged for the English title by William "Bendigo" Thompson. They met in February 1839 at Heather, Leicestershire with Bendigo taking the title in a tough battle, beating Burke after ten rounds on a foul. Burke then reclaimed the title after Bendigo retired in 1840 and he fought Nick Ward for the championship at Lillingstone Lovell, Buckinghamshire in September 1840 with Burke losing again on a foul in round seventeen.

James Burke's last fight was a win in thirty seven rounds against Bob Castles in June 1843 at Rainham Ferry, Essex, he then retired but died of consumption in extreme poverty in 1845 at the age of 35.

1828

Ned Murphy, Whetstone Common, Leics.	D	50r.	50min.	£14
George Murray, *unknown venue*	W		45min.	£24+purse
Thomas Hands. Old Oak Common, Acton, London	W	10r.	17min.	£24+purse
Massa Sambo, Old Oak Common, Acton, London	W	15r.	33min.	£24+purse

1829

Young Berridge, Leicester	W	11r.	22min.	£10+purse
Bill Fitzmaurice, Harpenden Common, Herts.	W	160r.	175min.	£50
Bill Cousens, Whetstone Common, Leics.	L	111r.	123min.	£20
Jem Girdler, Milford Bay, Northchapel, Sussex	W	17r.	39min.	£15+purse

1830

Andrew Gow, Temple Mills, London	W	22r.	25min.	£10
Bob Hampson, Hampden Common, London	W	41r.	44min.	£50
Tim Crawley, Whetstone Common, Leics.	W	34r.	30min.	£50

1831

David Davis, Shepperton Range, Middx.	W	12r.	27min.	£100
James Blissett, London	W	19r.	44min.	£50

1832

Jack Carter, Woolwich, London	W	11r.	25min.	£30+purse

1833

Harry Macone, Lockington Bottom, Beverley, Yorks.	W	59r.	98min.	£40

Claimed the Championship of England.

Simon Byrne, No Man's Land, London	W	99r.	186min.	£200

Retained the Championship.

1837

Samuel O'Rourke, New Orleans, USA (stopped by police)	D	3r.		$2000
Tom O'Connell, Hart's Island, New York, USA	W	10r.		$1000

Both these fights were claimed as for the Championship of America.

1839

William Thompson, Heather, Leics.	LF	10r.	24min.	£220

Lost the Championship of England but reclaimed the title after Thompson retired.

1840

Nick Ward, Lillingstone Level, Bucks.	L	17r.	138min.	£100

For the Championship of England.

1843

Bob Castles, Rainham Ferry, Essex	W	37r.	70min.	£50

The London Prize Ring Rules
1838
(Revised again in 1853)

The London Prize Ring Rules generally set out Broughton's Rules at greater length and in greater detail, specifying fouls more specifically. The main changes were:

1. The 'square of a yard' in Broughton's Rule 1 was replaced by the old 'scratch' line.

2. After the 30 seconds between rounds, and the umpire's call of 'Time', each man was required to walk to the scratch unaided and was allowed eight seconds to do so. This prevented the second from carrying boxers to the scratch who were, in reality, unfit to continue.

3. There was more attention paid to the boxers' dress, in particular limiting spikes on boots.

4. A man willfully going down without a blow was deemed to have lost the battle.

5. Fouls, such as butting, gouging, biting, scratching, kicking, the use of stones, etc. in the hand, squeezing on the ropes, were set out fully.

6. Provisions were made regarding wagers in the event of postponements, cancellations, interference by the law or darkness, boxers quitting the ring and other unforeseen circumstances.

William Thompson
(Champion of England 1839-1840 & 1845-1850)

Born: 1811   Died: 1880

"Bold Bendigo"

One of triplets born in Nottingham in 1811 and one of twenty one children altogether, he grew up to be an all-round athlete, excelling in boxing, athletics and acrobatics and became one of the most colourful characters of the prize ring. He stood 5' 9¾" and weighed somewhere between 164-168lbs. and possessed an extrovert personality which earned him his popularity in boxing, coupled with scientific skills, although he was also a member of the notorious "Nottingham Lambs", a gang of local louts.

His first twelve recorded fights against minor and mostly local opposition, from 1832-1834 all ended in wins for Bendigo, leading him to a grudge fight with his local and jealous arch enemy, the giant Ben Caunt. These two apparently genuinely hated each other and when they clashed in July 1835 in Nottingham, Caunt was disqualified after twenty two rounds of vicious brawling. After three more wins against Bill Brassey, Charles Langan and Bill Looney in 1836 and 1837, Bendigo again fought Ben Caunt in April of 1838 at Selby, Yorkshire, when again it was a vicious brawl, although this time Bendigo was disqualified after seventy five rounds and Ben Caunt was lucky to escape with his life after fighting broke out between his and Bendigo's supporters.

As James Burke, the Champion of England at the time was in America, Caunt claimed the championship, but this was not generally accepted, however Bendigo, who also recognized himself as a champion in waiting challenged Burke for the title when he returned to England and in February 1839 at Heather, Leicestershire, Bendigo took James Burke's crown when Burke was disqualified for a foul after ten rounds. Shortly after this fight Bendigo retired because being the showman he was, whilst entertaining a crowd with various party tricks he severely injured his knee while performing somersaults and landing awkwardly.

Bendigo stayed retired until 1845, but so much taunting and goading by Ben Caunt finally forced him to return to the prize ring where they squared up to each other, at Stony Stratford, near Milton Keynes, Buckinghamshire in September of that year. In another bloodthirsty contest in which all rules were broken once again, Caunt apparently went down without a blow being struck in round ninety three and was disqualified. Again riots broke out and again Ben Caunt had to flee for his life. Bendigo retired once more, only to be enticed back in 1850 at the age of 38 to fight Tom Paddock for the title at Mildenhall, Suffolk. Although he won on a disqualification in round forty nine, Bendigo took a beating from Paddock, a fighter not in the same class as Bendigo in his prime and after this fight Bendigo retired – this time for good.

He turned to drinking and brawling and by this time was also leader of the Nottingham Lambs, but after he had served his twenty eighth prison sentence for drunkenness and fighting he apparently saw the light and turned to religion becoming a preacher, touring all over the country trying to convince people of the errors of their ways as he had with fire and brimstone speeches, although he was apparently still partial to the odd tipple and a flutter on the horses! He died in 1880 aged 68.

1832

Joe Hanley	W	16r.
Bill Faulkner	W	11r.

1833

Ned Smith	W	5r.	
Charles Martin	W	2r.	5min.
Levi Jackson	W	3r.	
Tom Cox	W	9r	
George Skelton	W	3r.	
Tom Burton	W	9r.	
Bill Mason	W	3r.	
Bill Winterflood	W	1r.	
Bill Keyworth	W	11r.	

1834

The Bingham Champion	W

1835

Ben Caunt, Appleby House, Nottingham	WF	22r.	£50

1836
Bill Brassey, Deepcar, Sheffield WF 52r. £50

1837
Young Charles Langan, Woore, Newcastle W 32r. 93min. £50
Bill Looney, Chapel en le Frith, Derbys. W 99r. 144min. £200

1838
Ben Caunt, Skipworth Common, Yorks. LF 75r. 80min. £200
Claimed as for the Championship of England.

1839
James Burke, Heather, Leics. WF 10r. 24min. £220
Won the Championship of England.

1845
Ben Caunt, Stony Stratford, Milton Keynes WF 93r. 130min. £400
Retained the Championship.

1850
Tom Paddock, Mildenhall, Suffolk WF 49r. 59min. £400
Retained the Championship.

Ben Caunt
(Champion of England 1840-1841 & 1841-1845)

Born: 1815   Died: 1861

"The Torkard Giant"

Ben Caunt was born at Hucknall Torkard near Nottingham in 1815 and grew up to be a giant of a man at over 6' 2" tall and 210lbs. in weight. The son of a gamekeeper who worked for Lord Byron, Ben fought a few minor and unrecorded fights, but was jealous of the success and popularity of William "Bendigo" Thompson from nearby Nottingham. He challenged Bendigo and they met at Appleby House, Nottingham in July 1835, a vicious brawl ensued with Bendigo winning, as Caunt was disqualified after twenty two rounds for hitting during the interval.

Caunt then went on to beat William Butler in fourteen rounds at Stonyford, Nottinghamshire and Bill Boneford at Sunrise Hill, Nottingham in six rounds, both in 1837 before again meeting Bendigo in April 1838 at Selby, Yorkshire. This time Bendigo was disqualified in another disgraceful brawl, for going down without being hit in round seventy five, with Ben Caunt having to run for his life after crowd riots broke out between his supporters and Bendigo's supporters known as the Nottingham Lambs.

After beating Bill Brassey in one hundred and one rounds at Six Mile Bottom, Cambridgeshire, in October 1840, Caunt lost a title fight to the now recognized champion Nick Ward in seven rounds at Crookham Common, Newbury, Berkshire in February 1841. They met again in May of the same year at Long Marsden, Warwickshire, with Caunt beating Ward in a hard fought contest taking in thirty five rounds. Shortly after this fight Caunt sailed to America to challenge the American champion Tom Hyer, who was not interested in taking up the challenge, so Caunt returned six months later in in March 1842.

With the true champion and his bitter enemy, Bendigo in retirement, Ben Caunt successfully taunted and goaded him out of retirement for a third and decisive showdown in September, 1845 at

Stoney Stratford, near Milton Keynes. It was a brawl to end all brawls as every rule in the book was broken in a brutal and bloody affair, which ended in rather dubious fashion when, after ninety three rounds Caunt was disqualified, for apparently going down without being hit and Bendigo regained the title. Again Caunt had to flee for his life as rioting in the crowd broke out between the two sets of supporters. Ben Caunt fought only once more when he met Nat Langham, his brother-in-law, in a family feud fight in London in September 1857 and the pair fought out a draw when bad light finished the fight after sixty rounds.

When he retired he worked as a farm labourer before taking over the Coach & Horses pub in St. Martins Lane, London, making a very good living from it. In 1851 tragedy struck when he lost two of his children when the pub caught fire and he never really recovered from this tragedy dying in 1861.

1833-1834
Ben Caunt won several local contests including a win against George Graham, a potter from Lincolnshire.

1835

William Thompson, Appleby House, Nottingham	LF	22r.		£50

1837

William Butler, Stoneyford, Notts.	W	14r.		£40
Bill Boneford, Sunrise Hill, Notts.	W	6r.	12min.	£50

1838

William Thompson, Skipworth Common, Yorks.	WF	75r.	80min.	£200

Claimed as for the Championship of England.

1840

Bill Brassey, Six Mile Bottom, Cambs.	W	101r.	90min.	£200

Claimed as for the Championship of England.

1841

Nick Ward, Crookham Common, Berks.	LF	7r.	12min.	£200

For the Championship of England.

Nick Ward, Long Marsden, Warks.	W	35r.	47min.	£200

Won the Championship of England.

1845

William Thompson, Stoney Stratford, Bucks.	LF	93r.	130min.	£400

Lost the Championship.

1857

Nat Langham, Long Reach, Whitstable, Kent	D	60r.	89min.

Nick Ward
(Champion of England 1840)

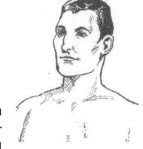

Born: 1811   Died: 1850

Nick Ward was born in London's East End in 1811 and was the younger brother of the former Champion of England, Jem Ward. At 6' 0" tall and weighing around 180lbs. Nick Ward trained to be a pugilist in one of the many sparring halls in London at that time. Having said that, he is rated as only an average fighter who although tricky and crafty, resorted to unfair tactics rather than face to face confrontation.

His first recorded fight was against John Lockyer in February 1835 at Moulsey Hurst, Surrey which he won in thirteen rounds, but his second fight against Sambo Sutton at Tottenham, London in May of that year ended in suspicious circumstances, with Ward mysteriously quitting in round twelve with rumblings in the fight fraternity of a fix. His next fight in October 1839, at Ditton Marshes, Kent against Jem Bailey was, for a time, halted by intervention of the law, however it continued with Ward winning in round thirty three on a foul.

In 1840 Ward met James Burke for the championship and with Burke suffering from a bad knee even before the fight started, Ward played a cruel cat and mouse game with him, making Burke come after him, knowing the longer the fight went, the worse it would be for Burke's injury. When Burke was sufficiently exhausted by his opponent's tactics, Ward hit him with several rights until Burke slumped to the ground. Confusion reigned as the crowd closed in but eventually Ward was given the decision, although it is believed Ward's gang had a lot to do with the positive result for him and making him the new Champion of England.

In February 1841 at Newbury, Berkshire, Nick Ward fought Ben Caunt for the coveted crown, where it is alleged that the crowd again had a controlling decision in the referee's decision to disqualify Caunt, for apparently hitting Ward while he was down, therefore allowing Nick Ward to retain the Champion of England title after seven rounds. A return contest was arranged immediately and in May of that year they met once again at Long Marsden, Warwickshire where Caunt beat an overweight Ward over thirty five rounds to regain the championship.

1835

John Lockyer, Moulsey Hurst, Surrey	W	18r.		£20
Sambo Sutton, Tottenham, London (fixed fight?)	L	12r.	30min.	£20+purse

1839

Jim Bailey, Woking Common, Surrey	WF	33r.	55min.	£50

1840

James Burke, Lillingstone Level, Oxon.	WF	17r.	138min.	£100

Won the Championship of England.

1841

Ben Caunt, Crookham Common, Berks.	WF	7r.	12min.	£200

Retained the Championship.

Ben Caunt, Long Marsden, Warwickshire	L	35r.	47min.	£200

Lost the Championship.

William Perry
(Champion of England 1850-1851)

Born: 1819   Died: 1881

"The Tipton Slasher"

William Perry was born in Tipton, Staffordshire in 1819 and moved to London when still a boy, working on the barges of the Thames and fighting in his spare time. His first known fight was against Barney Dogherty in November 1835, which ended when police intervened after seven rounds but resumed later the same day at a different venue with Perry winning after another six rounds.

Reputed to be over 6' 0" tall and weighing 190lbs. Perry or "The Slasher" as he was commonly known, possessed only average skills but was reputed to be clever and cool under pressure. In December 1836 he fought and beat Ben Spilsbury and then beat Jem Scunner in November 1837 over two consecutive days probably due to darkness falling on the first day of the fight or police interference. Perry then met the American giant, Charles Freeman and in their first meeting at Sawbridgeworth, Hertfordshire in December 1842, bad light stopped the fight after seventy rounds, so ending in a draw. The second meeting was decided two weeks later at Cliffe Marshes near Gravesend, Kent when Freeman won on a foul after thirty eight rounds after Perry apparently went down without being hit.

From 1843 to 1846 Perry fought Tass Parker on three occasions, firstly at Dartford, Kent in December 1843 when the law intervened after sixty seven rounds and the fight was declared a draw, secondly at Horley, Surrey in February 1844 when Parker was disqualified after a marathon one hundred and thirty three rounds and thirdly at Linderick Common in August 1846 when Parker was defeated in twenty three rounds. There were claims that these fights were for the championship, but this is probably not true; however with the true champion, the colourful Bendigo in retirement the position was confusing. It was a common ploy by pugilists to put forward their claims to being the champion to try to smoke out the recognized champion from inactivity or retirement while still holding on to the recognized title.

After Bendigo came out of retirement in 1850 to beat Tom Paddock and then retire for good, a title fight between Paddock and Perry was arranged and they met on Woking Common, Surrey in December of that year. Perry, a bigger man than Paddock was also much the better man and won the championship belt after the quick tempered Paddock was disqualified in round twenty seven, for apparently punching Perry while he was walking to his corner.

William Perry then next defended his title against Harry Broome at Newmarket, Suffolk in September 1851 and in a close fight which ended in round fifteen, Perry was disqualified for striking Broome when he was kneeling. Fights scheduled against Harry Broome in 1853 and Tom Paddock in 1856 were forfeited by these two fighters respectively. William Perry's last fight was against Tom Sayers in June 1857 at the Isle of Grain in the Medway Estuary, Kent with Perry losing in ten rounds and Sayers claiming the title. William Perry died suddenly in 1881 at the age of 61.

1835

Barney Dogherty, Mortlake, London (stopped by police)	D	7r.		£10
Barney Dogherty, Lechmore Common, Herts.	W	6r.		£10

1836

Ben Spilsbury, Oldsbury, Midlands	W	19r.	25min.	£20

1837

Jem Scunner, Gospel End, Staffs.	D	7r.		
Jem Scunner, Midlands Kingswood, Wolverhampton, West Midlands	W	31r.	60min.	£50

1838

John Farwall	W			

1842

Charles Freeman, Sawbridgeworth, Herts.	D	70r.	84min.	
Charles Freeman, Taplow Heath, Bucks	D	12r.		
Charles Freeman, Gravesend, Kent	LF	38r.	39min.	

1843

Tass Parker, Dartford Marshes, Kent (stopped by police)	D	67r.	94min.	£200

Claimed as for the Championship of England.

1844

Tass Parker, Horley, Surrey	WF	133r.	152min.	£100

Claimed as for the Championship of England.

1846
Tass Parker, Linderick Common, Midlands   WF   23r.   27min.   £200
Claimed as for the Championship of England.

1850
Tom Paddock, Woking Common, Surrey   WF   27r.   42min.   £200
Won the Championship of England.

1851
Harry Broome, Mildenhall, Suffolk   LF   15r.   33min.   £400
Lost the Championship.

1857
Tom Sayers, London area   L   10r.   102min.   £400
For the Championship of England.

1876
Sam Scott, Codfall Bridge   W   4r.   £4

Harry Broome
(Champion of England 1851-1856)

Born: 1826   Died: 1865

"The Unknown"

Born in Birmingham in 1826, Harry Broome was about 5' 10" in height and weighed around 168lbs. in his prime. He was taught to fight by his brother Johnny, who himself was a top class fighter, at his pub in Piccadilly, London. His first two recorded fights were in 1842 when he fought Byng Stocks in an exhibition bout and then winning against Hal Mitchell, where gloves or probably training mufflers were reputed to have been used for both fights.

In October 1843 he took on the tough as teak Fred "Bulldog" Mason at Northfleet, Kent and eventually won in thirty nine rounds, while in December, 1844 at Greenhithe, Kent against Joe Rowe, a crowd invasion forced a draw after eighty one rounds of fighting. In a rematch at Eynsham, Oxford in May 1845, Broome defeated Rowe in twenty seven rounds. Broome was involved in another disgraceful crowd invasion at his fight with Ben Terry at Shrivenham, Berkshire in February 1846 when after a bitter brawl the only thing that saved both fighters from disqualification was when the referee left the ring, probably for his own safety, without giving a decision; it is therefore credited as a draw.

In 1851 at Mildenhall, Suffolk, Harry Broome met William Perry, "The Tipton Slasher", for his championship title and removed it from him in round fifteen, when Perry was judged to have hit Broome while he was kneeling. This verdict was vehemently disputed by Perry, however Harry Broome was now recognized as the new champion. Broome agreed to then take on Harry Orme and they clashed at Brandon, Suffolk in April of that same year in what has been described as a fight which was a credit to the art of pugilism, with Broome retaining his title after thirty one rounds.

In May 1856, challenger Tom Paddock met Broome for the title near Ipswich and although Paddock was in fine condition and at the top of his game, Broome was vastly overweight and because of this he was so badly beaten after fifty one rounds that the sponge was thrown in and Tom Paddock was crowned the new Champion of England.

Harry Broome retired from the ring after the fight with Tom Paddock to run a pub, the Albion Tavern in Portsmouth and became involved in horse racing; however he was dead by the age of 39.

1842

Byng Stocks, London	EX			
Hal Mitchell, London (gloves)	W			£5+purse

1843

Fred Mason, Northfleet, Kent	W	39r.	81min.	£100

1844

Joe Rowe, Greenhithe. Kent	D	81r.	141min.	£100

The stakes were withdrawn when a mob broke into the ring.

1845

Joe Rowe, Ensham Common, Oxford	W	27r.	57min.	£100

1846

Ben Terry. Shrivenham, Berks.	D	49r.	65min.	£200

1851

William Perry, Mildenhall. Suffolk	WF	15r.	33min.	£400

Won the Championship of England.

1853

Harry Orme, Brandon, Essex	W	31r.	138min.	£500

Retained the championship.

1856

Tom Paddock, Manningtree, Essex	L	51r.	63min.	£400

Lost the Championship.

Tom Paddock
(Champion of England 1856-1858)

Born: 1824   Died: 1863

"The Redditch Needlepointer"

Born in 1824 on a farm near Redditch, Worcestershire, Paddock, although skilful and with plenty of stamina, he unfortunately suffered from a violent temper which resulted in fouling tactics in the ring on many occasions which marred his ring record to a certain extent. He stood 5' 10½" and weighed around 168lbs.

After a few minor local fights his first recorded contest was against Fred Pearce at Mapleborough Green, Warwickshire in January 1844, which he won after one and a half hours, he then proceeded to beat Jack Stagg, Elijah Parsons and Sam Hurst, all in that same year. He then fought Nobby Clarke twice, in January 1846 and in April 1847, beating him both times in forty two rounds and thirty five rounds respectively.

In 1850 at Mildenhall, Suffolk he contested the title with the now 39 year old Bendigo, the recognized champion who came out of retirement, but two reckless foul blows in round forty nine, when he was winning, cost the younger Paddock the fight. There was pandemonium after the fight however with Paddock losing his temper and giving Bendigo another thump, the crowd started to riot and one of Paddock's supporters also gave the referee a crack on the head with a blunt instrument!

Bendigo retired once again and it was decided that same year that Tom Paddock and William Perry should fight to decide the championship, this time on Woking Common, Surrey. Again Paddock's quick temper cost him the title when, after being knocked down by Perry, he jumped up and striking his opponent on the back of the neck as Perry was walking back to his corner after twenty seven rounds had been fought.

He lost again in a brutal bout over seventy one rounds against Harry Poulson in September 1851 at Sedgebrook, Lincolnshire and in the return fight in December of that year, although Paddock was giving Poulson a beating at the time, magistrates halted the contest after eighty six rounds by the law, a crowd riot followed the stoppage and one of the police officers was beaten unconscious. Both Paddock and Paulson were arrested and sentenced to ten months hard labour.

Illness then stopped Paddock fighting in 1852 and after taking 1853 off to regain his health and fitness, Paddock and Poulson, met once more at Mildenhall, Suffolk and in a terrific battle that lasted one hundred and two rounds, Poulson finally couldn't make it to the scratch and Paddock was declared the winner. In another savage fight five months later Paddock defeated Aaron Jones by knockout after a marathon one hundred and twenty one rounds of fighting with Jones eyes so bruised, cut and swollen they were just mere slits.

Later that year Paddock threw out a challenge for the championship, to both Harry Broome and William Perry, both refused so Paddock claimed the title anyway, although it was not generally recognized. Paddock again beat Aaron Jones in June 1855 and again declared himself the champion, to which Broome challenged Paddock to decide the rightful owner of the title. They met at Manningtree, Essex in May 1856 and in a one-sided fight Tom Paddock ended up undisputed Champion of England, beating Harry Broome in fifty one rounds. Broome played second fiddle to Paddock throughout a completely one-sided fight, ending up a physical wreck by the time Paddock finished him off with a powerful blow to the chest.

He briefly formed a travelling booth with Broome, but after a fairly successful tour Paddock then fell ill and into debt through losses on the racetrack and a fight with William Perry fell through because Paddock could not find a backer due to his health and penniless state even though he was the recognized champion.

Due to his money troubles it was an unfit Paddock who was forced to fight challenger Tom Sayers for the title in June 1858 on Canvey Island, Kent and was easily beaten in twenty one rounds, probably due to the fact that he was ring rusty, 34 years old and had just recovered from rheumatic fever. When, in November 1860 at Newbury, Berkshire and again ill and unfit, he was challenged by title contender, Sam Hurst, Paddock was knocked out cold in five rounds in a fight which only lasted about 10 minutes. He fought a few exhibition matches after that but after another long illness the brave and courageous Tom Paddock died in 1863 aged only 39 years old.

Prior to 1844
Tom Paddock won several minor local fights that were not recorded.

1844

Fred Pearce, Marpleborough Green, Midlands	W		90min.	£5+purse
Jack Stagg, *unknown venue*	W			
Elijah Parsons, Sutton Coldfield, Midlands	W	23r.	22min.	£40
Sam Hurst, Redditch, Midlands	W		25min.	£40

1846

Nobby Clarke, Coleshill Castle, Midlands	W	44r.	55min.	£50

1847

Nobby Clarke, Stoney Stratford, Bucks.	WF	35r.	48min.	£100

1850

William Thompson, Mildenhall, Suffolk	LF	49r.	59min.	£400
For the Championship of England.				
William Perry, Woking Common, Surrey	LF	27r.	42min.	£200
For the Championship of England.				

1851

Harry Poulson, Sedgebrook, Lincs.	L	71r.	95min.	£50
Harry Poulson, Belper, Derbys.	W	86r.	95min.	£100

1854

Harry Poulson, Mildenhall, East London	W	102r.	144min.	£200
Aaron Jones, Whitstable, Kent	W	121r.	144min.	£200
Claimed the Championship of England but not generally recognized.				

1855

Aaron Jones, Mildenhall, East London	W	61r.	89min.	£200
Claimed as for the Championship of England.				

1856

Harry Broome, Manningtree, Essex	W	51r.	63min	£400
Won the Championship of England.				

1858

Tom Sayers, Canvey Island, Kent	L	21r.	80min.	£300
Lost the Championship.				

1860

Sam Hurst, Newbury, Berks	L	5r.	10min.	£400
For the Championship of England.				

Tom Sayers
(Champion of England 1857-1860)

Born: 1826   Died: 1865

"The Brighton Boy"

Tom Sayers was born in a small cottage in the deprived slum district of Pimlico, Brighton, the youngest of five children, his father, James Sayers being a travelling cobbler. Tom received a brief education when he entered Middle Street School, Brighton, aged nine years in 1836, but at thirteen he left home to become an apprentice bricklayer in London, where he worked on the new London and North Western Railway Stations of King's Cross and St Pancras.

After a couple of fights in the Brighton area Tom Sayers first fight in London was against an Irish bricklayer colleague, apparently a grudge match caused by the Irishman's dislike of Tom's jokes. The fight on Wandsworth Common, London lasted up to two and a half hours, after which the young Sayers felled the 6' 3" Irishman. Sayers chose to fight barefoot, which gave him an advantage in the muddy conditions and his defeated opponent was carried away unconscious to a doctor, who later called the police. To escape arrest, Sayers fled back to Sussex, his reputation as a fighter now established, but he returned to London, continuing his day job as a labourer where he is known to have worked on the London Road Viaduct, which was completed in 1846. The amazing thing about Sayers was that he only stood 5' 8½" high and weighed 154lbs. at his heaviest, yet met and beat many men far heavier than himself with his speed and agility, coupled with a powerful punch in either fist.

In 1849 he advertised in the widely read "Bell's Life" magazine that he would take on all comers, which resulted in a win over Abe Crouch at Greenhithe, Kent in 1849. In 1850 he fought a draw with Dan Collins at Edenbridgel, Kent, with police at first stopping the first fight after nine rounds but they continued later that day fighting to a draw after another thirty nine rounds. Sayers then defeated Dan Collins in a rematch in 1851 at Long Reach, near Whitstable, Kent. Wins against Jack Grant and Jack Martin in June 1852 and January 1853 respectively, propelled Sayers forward later that year to a contest (Sayers was not fighting the heavier men at this time) against Nat Langham, who was generally considered to be the best of the middleweights in the land. Langham won convincingly after sixty one rounds in a tough fight at Lakenheath, Suffolk, although it is reported that Sayers may have been out of condition.

After beating George Sims in four rounds in February 1854, Sayers, unable to find men at middleweight to fight him began to take on heavier men like 168lb. Harry Poulson at Appledore, Kent in 1856, finally overcoming him after one hundred and nine rounds following this up with a draw and win respectively against Aaron Jones another much heavier man, in 1857. Later that year Sayers fought William Perry on the Isle of Grain, Kent defeating Perry in ten rounds and claiming the title of Champion of England, which he then defended this claim successfully against the virtual novice Bill Benjamin, beating him easily in three rounds.

When he defeated Tom Paddock at Canvey Island, Essex in June 1858 after twenty one rounds Sayers became the undisputed Champion of England. He followed this up with a return title fight against a much improved Bill Benjamin in April 1859 at Ashford, Kent, but still resulting in a comfortable win for Sayers after eleven rounds. Another comfortable seven round win against Bob Brettle who was also a middleweight like himself in September of that same year firmly established Sayers as a formidable pugilist in the middleweight division as well, although Sayers had long relinquished any interest to being described as the best of the middleweights. He preferred to be recognized as the king of the heavier weight and because of this it was Bob Brettle, who had already assumed this title, who was to fight Jem Mace twice for this claim.

Sayers was then challenged by the American Heavyweight Champion, John C. Heenan to decide who was best in what was described as for the Championship of the World, in a historic fight that was to become the best remembered contest for either fighter. This fight took place at Farnborough, Hampshire in April of 1860, and attracted thousands. After breaking his arm in the sixth round, Sayers fought a heroic defensive battle, although Heenan also had his problems with his left hand badly swollen by round twenty one and later having trouble with his eyesight as well. By this time the police were trying to jostle their way through the crowd to the ring to stop the fight and by round thirty seven the referee had also been separated from the fighters by the crowd pushing forward. The two men carried on until round forty two when the crowd finally spilled into the ring, leaving the two fighters no room to manoeuvre. The referee fought his way back to where Sayers and Heenan were and ordered the two pugilists to stop fighting and with that Heenan took off out of the ring, pushing his way through the throngs of spectators, only stopping when he fell down temporarily blind. There could be no other verdict from the referee apart from a draw in what was to be described as one of the great bare knuckle fights of the century and a month later both Tom Sayers and John C. Heenan both received a special silver championship belt to commemorate this memorable fight.

Tom Sayers never fought again, relinquishing his Champion of England title and after several failures in the world of business, his last years were spent as a sick man, dying of diabetes in 1865 at 39 years old, only five years after his historic fight with the American, John C. Heenan, but he will always be remembered for this fight.

1842-1844

Haines, near Brighton Racecourse (stopped by police)	D			
Wade, a labourer, East Sussex	W	6r.		
Unknown Irishman, Wandsworth, London	W		165min.	

1849

Abe Crouch, Greenhithe, Kent	W	6r.	13min.	

1850

Dan Collins, Edenbridge, Kent (stopped by police)	D	9r.	27min.	
Dan Collins, Redhill, Kent (same day as above)	D	39r.	112min	£50

1851

Dan Collins, Long Reach, Whitstable, Kent	W	44r.	84min.	£50

1852

Jack Grant, Mildenhall, Suffolk	W	64r.	150min.	£200

1853

Jack Martin, Long Reach, Whitstable, Kent	W	23r.	55min.	£100
Nat Langham, Lakenheath, Suffolk	L	61r.	122min.	£200

1854

George Sims, Long Reach, Whitstable, Kent	W	4r.	5min.	£75

1856

Harry Poulson, Appledore, Kent	W	109r.	188min.	£100

1857

Aaron Jones, Canvey Island, Essex (darkness fell)	D	62r.	180min.	£200
Aaron Jones, Medway, Kent	W	85r.	120min.	£200
William Perry, Isle of Grain, Kent	W	10r.	102min.	£400

Claimed as for the Championship of England.

1858

Bill Benjamin, Isle of Grain, Kent	W	21r.	80min.	£400

Claimed as for the Championship of England.

Tom Paddock, Canvey Island, Kent	W	21r.	80min.	£300

Won the Championship of England.

1859

Bill Benjamin, Ashford, Kent	W	11r.	22 min.	£400

Retained the Championship.

Bob Brettle, Leashford, Sussex	W	7r.	15min.	£600

Retained the Championship.

1860

John Heenan, Farnborough, Hants	D	42r.	138min.	£400

Billed as for the Championship of the World.

Sam Hurst
(Champion of England 1860-1861)

Born: 1832   Died: 1882

"The Stalybridge Infant"

Born in Stalybridge, Lancashire, Sam Hurst was known as the Stalybridge Infant, probably because he stood 6' 3" and weighed a massive 210lbs.-238lbs. He also had the unique record of becoming the Champion of England in his first fight, however he was better known as a wrestler rather than a boxer, in fact it was claimed he was the Champion of Lancashire at wrestling. He was a strong man, whose muscular frame was built up by working as a hammer striker in a local foundry and as a result of this his backer's, on Sam's behalf, cheekily put him forward as the rightful claimant to the now vacant title.

No one took any notice, including John C. Heenan, who like Tom Sayers had retired after their historic battle and because of this Sam Hurst was launched on a sparring tour around England, which only advertised his limited prowess as a boxer for all to see. In the end this stunt worked because Tom Paddock, the former champion, objected to a wrestler claiming a boxing title and so challenged him for the title vacated by the retirement of Tom Sayers. The fight took place on the Berkshire Downs, near Newbury in November 1860 and although unfit, sick and a debt-ridden man, Paddock began the fight easily the better man against the slow and cumbersome Hurst, winning the first two rounds comfortably. However, in the third round Hurst caught Paddock with a sucker punch described at the time as a terrific roundhouse hammer blow to the body, which lifted Paddock clean off his feet and so it was curtains for poor old Tom, whose seconds threw in the sponge immediately, as Hurst had broken three of Paddock's ribs with that punch. Sam Hurst in his first professional fight was the new Champion of England! After this farce of a fight no one came forward to challenge Hurst, which in a way was lucky for him as he broke his ankle in a wrestling match shortly after!

In June 1861 came a surprise challenge from Jem Mace, it was a surprise because at six inches shorter and about 70 pounds lighter in weight, no one gave Mace, although a fine fighter, a chance against the bigger and stronger Sam Hurst. The contest held by the side of the River Medway, Kent was one sided, but not as expected, because it was Jem Mace's speed and punching that beat the awkward and ponderous Sam Hurst into a total mess. His top lip was split open to his nose, his left ear became the size of a cricket ball and pouring with blood and his eyes almost closed. In the end Hurst's seconds, Jem Hodgkiss and Jerry Noon would not allow him to continue taking further punishment after a brutal eight rounds.

Sam Hurst never fought as a pugilist again, although he did for some time afterwards continue as a wrestler with some success. He died at the age of 50 in 1882.

Undated
Smith, Deansgate, Manchester   W   2r.

1860
Tom Paddock, near Newbury, Berks.   W   5r.   10min.   £400
Won the Championship of England.

1861
Jem Mace, Home Circuit, Medway, Kent   L   8r.   40min.   £400
Lost the Championship.

Jem Mace
(Champion of England 1861-1862 & 1863-1871)

Born: 1831 Died: 1910

"The Swaffham Gypsy"

Jem Mace was born in Beeston, Norfolk in 1831, the son of a blacksmith and one of four brothers and learned how to box as a boy. Standing only 5' 9" tall and weighing at his heaviest fighting weight 175lbs. Jem Mace was probably the most scientific boxer in the history of the English prize ring, with a technique that was the forerunner of the styles seen in the ring to this day. He could hit very hard with both fists, attack and defend with skill, was light on his feet and was able to adapt his style and fight game to the styles of his opponents.

His first recorded fight was against Sidney Smith at Wisbech, Cambridgeshire, winning in two hours and he followed this up with wins against Charlie Pinfold in four rounds, Farden Smith and Tom Brewer, but the following year lost to John Pratt, however he reversed that decision the next year. In 1852 he beat Tom Harvey at Norwich, while in 1853 his record only shows a couple of minor fights against a certain Gutteridge of Godstone and someone called Nickels. In 1855 at Mildenhall, Suffolk Mace defeated Bob Slack of Norwich in nine rounds.

It was then Mace decided to move to London where the bigger fights and purses were, meeting Bill Thorpe at Canvey Island, Essex in 1857 and winning in eighteen rounds. Twice, once in 1857 and then in 1858, a contest against Mike Madden failed to come off, however a fight with Bob Brettle, then considered the premier middleweight was arranged at the Medway, Kent, but in a very poor showing by the Norfolk man, Bob Brettle defeated him in just two rounds and although both men always denied it, many people thought the fight was fixed. In 1859 Jem Mace took on the dangerous Ned "Posh" Price at Aldershot, Hampshire, beating Price in eleven rounds and followed this up with a hard fought win by disqualification over Bob Travers in 1860. A return against Bob Brettle concluded in an emphatic win for Mace when first at Wallingford, Berkshire where the fight was interrupted by the law, Mace finished off Brettle the next day at Foulness Island, Essex in five rounds and with it gaining recognition as the best middleweight in the land.

Having put on weight and wanting to go after the holy grail of prize fighting, Mace took on the giant Sam Hurst for the Championship of England in June 1861, stopping him in eight rounds near Southend, Essex. Tom King who was ringside immediately challenged Mace and so in January 1862 at Godstone, Kent they faced each other and although King floored Mace in round twenty seven, Mace recovered to flatten King in round forty three. In a return fight on the Medway, Kent in November 1862, King stopped Mace in round twenty one to exact revenge and gain the title. Mace then reclaimed the title back after King retired. The next year, 1863 saw Mace defend his crown against Joe Goss at Wootten Bassett, Wiltshire, but police intervened after one round and the fight was transferred to Plumstead, London later that day, with Mace coming out on top after nineteen rounds.

In August 1866 after police again intervened in a fight against Joe Goss for the Championship of England, Mace finally overcame Goss with a twenty one round win and then set sail for America in 1869 where he hammered the unbeaten American champion Tom Allen to defeat in ten rounds in May 1870. In May 1871 in what is generally described as a world title fight he fought Joe Coburn, but police intervened, so they fought again, this time to a draw, near St. Louis with Mace being shot at after the fight!

Mace returned to England entering into exhibition bouts the length and breadth of the country against the likes of Herbert Slade, Charlie Mitchell and Jack Smith. He then set sail for Australia in 1877 with his own travelling boxing booth, where he passed on his knowledge and experience and taking on exhibition bouts and then on to New Zealand where again he ran his own boxing booths, teaching local fighters his extensive skills of the noble art and again taking part in many exhibition bouts.

On his return to England in 1883 Mace carried on the exhibition bouts until challenged by Charlie Mitchell, after Mace apparently made disparaging remarks about Mitchell, who took exception to these slurs and in February 1890 in Glasgow, Mace who was now 59 was defeated in four rounds.

Even in the 1890's when he was in his sixties Jem Mace still fought exhibition bouts with other veteran pugilists such as Bob Travers. Jem Mace won a fortune in the ring and lost it outside the ring due mainly to his gambling habit and when with a travelling fair near Jarrow, County Durham, the great Jem Mace was taken ill and died at the age of 79 in 1910.

With the bare knuckle era now coming to an end and the advent of the Queensbury Rules in 1867, many of the bare knuckle fighters that were left emigrated to America where it still had a big following and also where bigger purses could be earned.

Jem Mace is considered by many to be one of the last bare knuckle fighters, even though a lot of his fights were fought with gloves, which he preferred and encouraged. He is also considered the father of boxing as we know it today and was a wonderful ambassador for the sport taking his unique skills and knowledge all over the world.

1849

Sydney Smith, Wisbech, Cambs.	W		120min.	£10
Charlie Pinfold, Norwich, Norfolk	W	4r.		
Tom Brewer, Horncastle, Lincs. (gloves)	W		110min.	
Farden Smith, Norwich, Norfolk	W	5r.		

1850

John Pratt, Drayton, Norfolk	L	50r.	130min.	£20

1851

John Pratt, Drayton, Norfolk	W	8r.	29min.	

1852

Tom Harvey, Norwich, Norfolk	W	31r.	60min.	purse

1853

Gutteridge of Godstone	W			
Nickels	L			

1855

Bob Slack, Mildenhall, Suffolk	W	9r.	19min.	£10

1857

Bill Thorpe, Canvey Island, Essex	W	18r.	27min.	£50

1858

Bob Brettle, Medway, Kent	L	2r.	3min.	£200

Recognized as for the best middleweight in the country.

1859

Ned "Posh" Price, Aldershot, Hants.	W	11r.	17min.	£100

1860

Bob Travers, Kent Marshes, Kent (stopped by police)	D	6r.	21min.	
Bob Travers, Kent Marshes, Kent	WF	57r.	91min.	£100
Bob Brettle, Wallingford, Oxon. (stopped by police)	D	6r.	12min.	
Bob Brettle, Foulness Island, Essex	W	5r.	7min.	£400

Won the Middleweight Championship.

1861

Sam Hurst, Medway, Kent	W	8r.	50min.	£400

Won the Championship of England.

1862

Tom King, Godstone, Surrey	W	43r.	68min.	£400

Retained the Championship.

Tom King, Medway, Kent	L	21r.	38min.	£400

Lost the Championship.

1863

Joe Goss, Wootten Bassett, Wilts. (stopped by police)	D	1r.	4min.	
Plumstead, Kent (resumed same day)	W	19r.	115min.	

Regained the Championship.

1866

Joe Goss, Meopham, Kent	D	1r.	65min.	£400

Due to a dispute neither fighter threw a punch throughout so referee abandoned the contest.

Joe Goss, Purfleet, Essex	W	21r.	31min.	£400

1870

Tom Allen, Kennerville. Louisiana, USA	W	10r.	44min.	$5,000

Claimed as for the Championship of the World.

1871

Joe Coburn, Port Ryeson, Canada	D	1r.	77min.	$5,000

No punches were thrown, the police arrived, the fight was abandoned and rescheduled for a later date.

Joe Coburn, St. Louis, Missisippi, USA	D	12r.	208min.	$10,000

Retained the Championship of the World.

1876

Bill Davis, Virginia City, Nevada, USA	W	8r.

1877

Bill Davis, San Francisco, California, USA	WKO	4r.

1890

Charlie Mitchell, Glasgow, Scotland	ND	4r.

1896

Mike Donovan, New York, USA	D	6r.

Veterans Championship of the World.

1897
Mike Donovan, Birmingham, Midlands   D   6r.
Veterans Championship of the World.

Because Jem Mace took part in so many exhibition fights in England, USA, Australia, New Zealand and South Africa from 1868 onwards, only his competitive fights are listed here.

Tom King
(Champion of England 1862-1863)

Born: 1835 Died: 1888

"The Fighting Sailor"

Tom King was born in Stepney, East London in 1835, growing up to work in the docks and then going to sea. Trained by Jem Mace he possessed good boxing skills coupled with being strong, fast and with good stamina. He was 6' 2" in height and weighed in the region of 182lbs. King's first known fight was against a certain Bill Clamp in 1859 which he won in the first round and then in 1860 he beat Brighton Bill also in the first round. In November 1860 against Tom Truckle at Kentish Marshes he won after forty nine rounds in just over an hour and in October 1861 he fought a brutal contest against Young Broome (William Evans), but police intervened at the venue in Farnborough, Hampshire after seventeen rounds. In time honoured tradition the fight moved over the border into Surrey, where it continued until King eventually won in twenty six rounds.

Tom King then challenged Jem Mace for the championship in January 1862 but was knocked out cold by Mace in forty three rounds at Godstone, Surrey, however in a return fight on the Medway in November of that same year, King had his revenge and gained the heavyweight belt when stopping Mace in twenty one rounds with a terrific right hand hammer punch.

He then retired, but John C. Heenan, the American, had the temerity to claim the Championship of England and so like any upstanding patriot, King would not stand for a usurper claiming our crown, so King changed his mind and came out of retirement. They met in December 1863 at Wadhurst, Sussex, where they contested a pretty even fight until round eighteen, after which, by then, Heenan was so badly weakened and King finished him off in the round twenty four. King then retired for a second and last time, eventually to go on to make a fortune, betting on the horses and indulging in his passion for sculling. He was also a very good and knowledgeable gardener who specialized in growing roses.

Tom King died in 1888 at the age of 59 a very rich man.

1859

Bill Clamp (Dockyard Champion)	W	1r.		

1860

Brighton Bill, Plaistow Marshes, London	W	1r.		
Tom Truckle, Kentish Marshes	W	49r.	62min.	£100

1861

Young Broome, Farnborough, Hants. (stopped by police)	D	17r.	20min.	
Fight resumed same day	W	26r.	22min.	£100

1862

Jem Mace, Godstone, Surrey	L	43r.	68min.	£400
For the Championship of England.				
Jem Mace, Medway, Kent	W	21r.	38min	£400
Won the Championship of England.				

1863

John Heenan,Wadhurst, Kent	W	24r.	35min.	£2000
Retained the Championship and claimed the World title.				

Joe Wormald
(Champion of England 1865-1868)

Born: 1840   Died: 1871

Joe Wormald was born in Poplar, London and not a lot is known about his growing years in the capital. He was reputed to be of low intelligence, however boxing records describe him as a fine boxer, being skilful, fast, strong and durable, standing just under 6' tall and weighing from 168lbs.-189lbs. throughout his career.

Jem Mace, at the time still the recognized champion did not rate Wormald's skill that highly and although he remained unbeaten, his record is not really that impressive considering he was involved in just as many no contests as fights.

His first recorded fight in 1863 on Rainham Marshes, Essex against journeyman Jack Smith ended in a draw after one hundred and thirteen rounds when darkness beat them and the stakes withdrawn. His next fight against the durable George Iles of Bristol was more successful for Wormald, winning in twenty four rounds but took just over two hours in a tough contest.

With Jem Mace, the recognized champion inactive for two years, Wormald was matched against the promising Andrew Marsden at Horley, Surrey and won in eighteen rounds in a fight lasting thirty seven minutes, which had Joe Wormald claiming the championship belt. Mace obviously upset at this young usurper, challenged Wormald and articles were signed, but Wormald cried off at the last minute with a supposed arm injury. Two years later the tables were reversed when Ned O'Baldwin arrived late for their championship fight and forfeited the title to Wormald. They did meet the next year, 1867, in America, in a bout billed as for the English title but the police intervened and although O'Baldwin was caught and jailed, Wormald managed to escape to Canada. In Montreal he opened a boxing saloon which became a success, so he opened another one in Quebec in 1870, however Wormald became ill and was sent to an asylum, where he died the following year.

1857

Walker of Plymouth	W	7r.	30min.

1863
Jack Smith, Rainham Marshes, Essex   D   113r.   265min.   £50
  (darkness fell)

1864
George Iles, London area   W   24r.   128min.   £5

1865
Andrew Marsden, Horley, Surrey   W   18r.   37min.   £400
Claimed the Championship of England.

1868
Ned Baldwin, Mass., USA (stopped by police)   D   1r.   10min. $2000
Retained the Championship (the English title, although fought for in the USA).

From about 1870 many of the boxers were fighting with gloves or emigrating to America where bare knuckle fighting was still popular. Jem Smith is generally regarded as the last English prize ring champion to participate in bare knuckle fights although later he mainly fought with gloves.

THE MIDDLEWEIGHTS

With a weight range of approximately 140lbs.-166lbs. the first men of any significance in this weight class were Daniel Mendoza and Richard Humphries in the 1780's and 1790's, particularly Mendoza who fought Humphries three times, but who had to take on much heavier men most of the time to attract fights. In fact Mendoza was considered to be the Champion of England between the years 1794-1795.

Tom Belcher was probably the first to be generally acclaimed as the best in the land at a "middle" weight when successful smaller men began to participate more in prize fighting at the end of the 18th century and the beginning of the 19th century. Belcher was beaten by Dutch Sam in 1806, but Dutch Sam never laid claim to any accolade, so Belcher still held this distinction.

This recognized weight class filled the void between lightweights and Champions of England and the word middleweight came into popular usage from the 1850's to describe pugilists of this weight.

Tom Belcher
(Acclaimed as the best in the land at a middle weight 1805-1813)

Born: 1783   Died: 1854

Born in the city of Bristol and in his prime standing 5' 9" in height and weighing about 154lbs. Tom Belcher was considered the most skilful boxer in the land at the time. He followed his brothers Ned and Jem to London in 1803 where his first recorded fight in June 1804 at Tooting Fields, London was against Jack Warr the son of the former fighter Bill Warr, who had lost to Daniel Mendoza for the Championship of England in 1794. Tom Belcher won in nineteen hard fought rounds, knocking out Warr who was carried out of the ring unconscious by his supporters. He surprisingly lost his next fight when matched against Bill Ryan, the self-acclaimed Irish champion, at Willesden Green, London in thirty eight rounds, but then beat the highly rated Jack O'Donnell at Shepperton Common, London before winning a return contest with Bill Ryan with ease.

Already he was being touted as the best in the land at middleweight when, in April 1806 at Sandon Heath, Thorpe, Surrey the still relatively inexperienced Tom Belcher was pitched in with the great Dutch Sam, claimed by most as the top lightweight in the country and certainly pound for pound the hardest puncher of all the prize ring pugilists around at that time. However it took Sam fifty seven rounds before Tom Belcher's seconds threw in the sponge, to stop their man taking further punishment, but because of this brave showing by Belcher a rematch was arranged for July 1807 at Moulsey Hurst, Surrey. In a bruising battle, Belcher with his left eye closed and Dutch Sam suffering from swollen eyes, bleeding nose and facial cuts battled away with neither giving ground. The fight ended in controversy when Belcher's camp accused Dutch Sam of a foul blow and although not conclusively proven, the final result was given firstly as a victory to Sam but after further consideration and several angry meetings it was declared a draw. Less than a month later they met for a third time at Lowfield Common, Sussex and in another bruising battle the harder punching power of Dutch Sam eventually got the better of Tom Belcher after thirty six rounds. Dutch Sam never claimed to be the best at middleweight after this win, although many recognized him as the best lightweight and now middleweight in the land at this particular time, so because of this, Belcher was still judged as the man to beat to assume this accolade.

Tom Belcher then went on to fight and easily beat Irishman Dan Dogherty whose backer Captain Fitzgerald threw in the sponge for his man after thirty three rounds at Epsom Downs in April 1808. Bill Cropley was Belcher's next opponent when they squared up at Mousley Hurst, Surrey in October 1808, Cropley collapsing with exhaustion in thirty four rounds. In February 1809, returning to Epsom Downs Belcher severely punished the completely outclassed Stephen Farnborough in less than 20 minutes. With Dutch Sam retiring in 1810 Tom Belcher was still considered by the majority as the best at middleweight in England and in June 1811 at Crawley Heath, Sussex in what was a total mismatch he knocked out George Silverthorne in seven rounds at Crawley Heath, Sussex.

In 1813 Belcher toured the country taking part in exhibition fights and then to Ireland, where he was challenged by an old adversary from five years before, Dan Dogherty, who now considered himself the best at middleweight in Ireland; so it was at the Curragh of Kildare that they faced each other in April of that same year with Belcher 14lbs. lighter than his opponent. Dogherty was still no match for Tom Belcher and after 35 minutes was knocked clean out. With this fight Belcher retired from the ring, although at a dinner he was attending in 1822, the rather inebriated and one time highly rated pugilist Jack Scroggins challenged Belcher, who, at 42 of age showed he had lost none of his skills when forcing the younger man to give in after 20 minutes, in a back room at the Castle Tavern pub in Holborn, London.

He later owned the Castle Tavern pub for fourteen years before finally returning to his home town of Bristol where he died in 1854 at the age of 71.

1804

Jack Warr, Tothill Fields, London	W	19r.	33 min.	50gns.
Bill Ryan, Willesden Green, London	L	38r.		£100+purse

1805

Jack O'Donnell, Shepperton Common, Surrey	W	15r.		20gns+purse
Bill Ryan, Chertsey, Surrey	W	29r.	50 min.	50gns.

Now regarded as best middleweight in the country.

1806

Dutch Sam, Moulsey Hurst, Surrey	L	57r.		100gns.
John Redding	W			£10

1807

Dutch Sam, Moulsey Hurst, Surrey	D	34r.		200gns.
Dutch Sam, Lowfield Common, Sussex	L	36r.	56min.	200gns.

Belcher still considered as best middleweight in the country as Dutch Sam never laid a claim to any title or accolade.

1808

Dan Dogherty, Epsom Downs, Surrey	W	33r.	45min.	10gns.
Bill Cropley,Moulsey Hurst, Surrey	W	34r.	56min.	50gns.+purse

1809

Stephen Farnborough, Epsom Downs, Surrey	W	8r.	20min.	£350

1811

George Silverthorn, Crawley Heath, Sussex	W	7r.	19min	£100+ purse

1813

Dan Dogherty, Curragh of Kildare, Ireland	W	26r.	35min.	£100+purse

1822

Jack Scroggins, Castle Tavern, London (turn-up)	W	5r.	20min.

Jack Scroggins
(Ring career 1803-1822)

Born: 1787   Died: 1836

"Scroggy"

Born in Deptford, London by the name of John
Palmer he apparently earned the nickname
through his many turn-ups with the boys of New
Cross, London as he was growing up. Fully grown he stood 5' 4" and
weighed between 144lbs.-152lbs. and was described as durable,
tough, and very argumentative, always up for a fight, although a
crude fighter; however he became one of the best and most colourful
middleweights of that era. Many of his early fights dating from 1803
and 1804 were against bigger and older youths and men and
according to the sketchy records from that time Jack Scroggins won
all of them!

Sometime after 1804 he was press-ganged into the navy after an
altercation with a law officer in London and his successful fighting
ways continued aboard ship and when on land, against fellow sailors
or local challengers. After eventually leaving the navy Jack Scroggins
first known involvement in a paid fight was against the experienced
Jack Boots at Willesden Green, London in 1814, which he won after
65 minutes of brutal fighting. The next year he was pitched in with
the battle hardened fellow Londoner, "Dolly" Smith at Coombe
Warren, South London and after 45 minutes Jack Scroggins was
again proved the winner when it was decided that Smith had taken
enough punishment.

He was now attracting some attention from the Fancy of the London
Prize Ring and was next matched, in that same year, against Bill
Nosworthy, whose claim to fame was beating the now gin soaked ring
legend Dutch Sam a year earlier. Nosworthy put up a brave fight but
was still outclassed and battered to defeat in fifteen rounds by the
rock hard fists of Jack Scroggins at Moulsey Hurst, Surrey. Later that
year the clever Bill Eales was Scroggins next opponent when they
met at Coombe Warren in a contest where the taller and heavier Eales
had the better of most rounds up until about round fourteen, then with

the heat of the day beginning to sap Eales's strength, Jack Scroggins took over and floored his opponent in round twenty three.

Scroggins did not fight again until 1816 when, after a dispute with a novice fighter, Bob Whitaker they confronted each other at Moulsey Hurst, Surrey. Out of condition Scroggy underestimated his adversary and nearly paid the price of over confidence, but eventually emerged the winner after forty nine rounds. Three months later Scroggins took on Joe Church the self-acclaimed Champion of Gloucestershire, again at Moulsey Hurst and in an epic battle in which both men took heavy punishment, Jack Scroggins again emerged the winner after fifty rounds.

The unbeaten Ned Turner, another highly rated middleweight was now offered up to the also unbeaten Jack Scroggins, for a fight which all the Fancy wanted to see. It came off at Hayes Turnpike, Middlesex in 1817, in front of an estimated twenty thousand spectators who came from far and wide travelling on all forms of transport and also on foot, but after four rounds the ring was broken by fans and the fight declared a draw. A return was arranged for three months later at Sawbridgeworth, Hertfordshire between these two top warriors. In front of another enormous crowd, Scroggins started well, but his bull like rushes were soon picked off by the more scientific Turner and he was heavily punished to the extent that after thirty three rounds he had to give in. Another contest was arranged between the two boxers the following year at Shepperton, Surrey and again Ned Turner proved to be the better man when Jack Scroggins admitted defeat after another brutal thirty nine rounds.

It was the beginning of the end now for Scroggins, after two successive defeats to Turner he now lost his next four fights, to highly rated Jack Martin, also in 1818, Josh Hudson in 1819 and twice to Josh's brother, David Hudson in 1820. Still game to fight on, although drinking heavily by now, he won a room fight against Harry Holt in 1821 after a celebratory dinner, both men drunk and unfit. He got himself into top condition later that year though, for a battle against Joe Parish at Banstead, Surrey which he won after sixty nine rounds, but from then on the end of his fighting career was close. Apart from a room fight he picked in a drunken state in 1822 against Tom Belcher, at the Castle Tavern, which he lost in fiverounds, his last fight was a seventeen round loss to Gypsy Jack Cooper at

Moulsey Hurst, Surrey later that year, Jack Scroggins was now finished as a prize fighter.

Losing all his hard earned money through alcohol, he now begged friends for food and drinks, he became destitute and a complete bore to anyone in the vicinity of a pub bar, who had to endure all his past ring exploits in slurred and probably exaggerated detail thrust upon them, until his demise in 1836.

1803

"Brickie Wilson, Appleton, Kent	W		65min.	
Bill Walters, Brentford, London	W		60min.	
Sam Beak, Sunbury Common, Surrey	W			
The Brickmaker, Appleton, Kent	W			
Long Will, Harrow, London	W			
Burke Smith, Cowley, Oxon.	W			

1804

Gypsy Bill Lee, Kilburn, London	W			
"No-Nose Blink, Kilburn, London	W			
Bill King, Sandford Green, Oxon.	W			
Jack Matney, Appleton, Kent	W			

Sometime after this Jack Scroggins was press-ganged into the Royal Navy.

1812

Dick Whalley, Harrow Road	W			

1814

Jack Boots, Willesdon Green, London	W		65min.	4gns.+purse

1815

"Dolly" Smith, Coombe Warren, Surrey	W		45min.	40gns.
Bill Nosworthy, Moulsey Hurst, Surrey	W	15r.	78min.	£100
Bill Eales, Coombe Warren, Surrey	W	23r.	22min.	50gns.

1816

Bob Whitaker, Moulsey Hurst, Surrey	W	49r.	76min.	100gns.
Joe Church, Moulsey Hurst, Surrey	W	50r.	58min.	200gns.

1817

Ned Turner, Hayes Turnpike, Middx.	D	4r.	25min.	150gns.
Young Fisher, Peter Street (room-fight) London	W	44r.	4 min.	40gns.
Ned Turner, Sawbridgeworth, Herts.	L	33r	72min.	200gns.

1818

Ned Turner, Shepperton, Surrey	L	39r.	91min.	£300
Jack Martin, Moulsey Hurst, Surrey	L	65r.	122min.	£250

1819

Josh Hudson, Moulsey Hurst, Surrey	L	11r.	18min.	25gns.

1820

David Hudson, Dagenham, Essex	L	34r.	40 min.	100gns.
David Hudson, Chelmsford Races	L	19r.	25 min.	£20+purse
Harry Holt, London (room-fight)	W	33r.	100 min.	10gns.

1821

Joe Parish, Banstead, Surrey	W	69r.	75 min.	50gns.

1822

Tom Belcher,Castle Tavern, London (room-fight)	L	5r.	20 min.	
Gypsy Jack Cooper, Moulsey Hurst Surrey	L	17r.	25 min.	£20

Ned Turner
(Ring career 1810-1824)

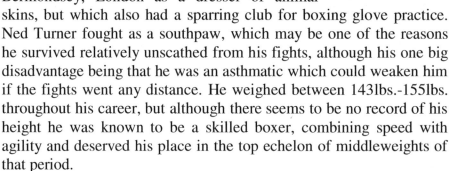

Born: 1791   Died: 1826

Born in Southwark, London of Welsh parents and grew up to be apprenticed at a yard in Bermondsey, London as a dresser of animal skins, but which also had a sparring club for boxing glove practice. Ned Turner fought as a southpaw, which may be one of the reasons he survived relatively unscathed from his fights, although his one big disadvantage being that he was an asthmatic which could weaken him if the fights went any distance. He weighed between 143lbs.-155lbs. throughout his career, but although there seems to be no record of his height he was known to be a skilled boxer, combining speed with agility and deserved his place in the top echelon of middleweights of that period.

His first recorded fight in 1810 was against a workmate John Balch, which he won in 50 minutes of hard fighting, although with or without gloves is not known. Turner's first paid fight in 1813 was in Locks Fields, London against a big unknown Irishman. John Keating, a local publican nominated Turner to challenge the Irishman which Ned Turner won in 25 minutes. In 1814 his day job then took him to Glasgow, Scotland where he also participated in a fight with Alec McNeil being the victor after 30 minutes and then on to work in Newcastle in 1816, where again he was successful in a contest against the much bigger "Slater" Blackett.

His first contest of any real note was later in 1816 and ended in tragedy, against Jack Curtis, older brother of the future brilliant lightweight champion, Dick Curtis. Unfortunately for Curtis, who was urged on by his seconds to carry on long after he was a beaten man, death occurred a few hours after their fight ended, due to the unnecessary punishment he had taken. Turner was found guilty of manslaughter instead of deliberate murder and spent two months in jail. After his release he won a fight against a Jewish pugilist by the name of Youler in 35 minutes in St. George's Fields, London.

At a dinner in February 1817, an argument between Jack Scroggins and Ned Turner resulted in a fight being made for the next month near Hayes, Middlesex and the fight was pretty even for the first four rounds, however part of the large crowd estimated at 30,000 invaded the ring and the contest had to be halted. A new match was made for three months later where a superior and still unbeaten Ned Turner beat a game, durable and to that point, unbeaten Jack Scroggins in thirty three rounds in just over an hour of fighting. After beating Jack Scroggins again in thirty nine rounds at Shepperton, Hertfordshire in October, 1818 in a battle in which his opponent put up another brave and mostly rearguard action, Ned Turner was now generally regarded as the leading middleweight in England around about this period, apart from Jack Randall, but Turner unfortunately came up against Randall only seven weeks after beating Jack Scroggins, in December of that year at Crawley Downs, Sussex. Even to start with and with both fighters throwing heavy blows, Turner started to gradually tire and by round thirty one he was almost out of it, finally having to submit three rounds later.

Ned Turner later went on to fight and beat the redoubtable Cy Davis on Wallingham Common, Surrey in 1819 in a fight he never looked like losing and then went on to beat highly rated Jack Martin, again the venue being Wallingham Common, the same Jack Martin who had also been beaten by the great Jack Randall. He fought Martin again in June 1821 at Crawley Downs but after 90 minutes of a bruising battle Ned Turner had to finally give in to the superior hitting power of Jack Martin after sixty rounds. A return with Cy Davis at Harpenden Common in 1823 also ended in defeat for Turner in eighteen rounds, although after being beaten by Peace Inglis at Colnbook Buckinghamshire in forty seven rounds in 1824, he avenged this loss by defeating Peace Inglis at the same venue seven months later, after breaking a bone in his hand in an earlier round, which eventually took him fifteen rounds to dispose of the brave but outfought Inglis. This was to be Ned Turner's last appearance in the prize ring which he had graced for the last eight years.

With his health fast deteriorating a benefit was organized in 1826, but Ned Turner died the evening before the event was due to take place.

1810

John Balch, Bermondsey, London	W	50 min.	

1813

Unknown Irishman, Lock's Fields, London	W	25 min.	10gns.

1814

Alec McNeil, Glasgow, Scotland	W		30min.	10gns.

1816

"Slater" Blackett, Newcastle-on-Tyne	W		45min.	
Jack Curtis, Moulsey Hurst, Surrey	W	68r.	85min.	100gns.
"Jew" Youler, St. George's Field, London	W		35 min.	

1817

Jack Scroggins, Hayes, Middx.	D	4r.	25min.	£150
Jack Scroggins, Sawbridgeworth, Herts.	W	33r.	72min.	£200

1818

Jack Scroggins, Shepperton, Herts.	W	39r.	91min.	300gns.
Jack Randall, Crawley Hurst, Sussex	L	34r.	39min.	£200

1819

Cy Davis, Wallingham Common, Surrey	W	32r.	45min.	200gns.
Jack Martin, Wallingham Common, Surrey	W	60r.	88min.	200gns.

1820

Josh Hudson, Lincoln Inn Fields, London (turn-up)	W	15min.	

1821

Jack Martin, Crawley, Sussex	L	60r.	80min.	£100

1823

Cy Davis, Harpenden Common, Herts.	L	18r.	35min.	£100

1824

Peace Inglis, Colnbrook, Bucks.	L	47r.	78min.	£100
Peace Inglis, Colnbrook, Bucks.	W	15r.	46min.	£100

111

Jack Randall
(Acclaimed as the best in the land at a middle weight 1817-1821)

Born: 1794   Died: 1828

"The Nonpareil"

Born in St. Giles, London, in a slum area, Jack Randall grew up to become one of the all-time great bare knuckle prize fighters, starting off as a lightweight and then moving into the middleweight division. He stood 5' 6" in height and weighed around 147lbs. He was involved in many street fights from an early age which stood him in good stead for the future, but over the years he harnessed this aggression and as a twenty year old he beat Jack Payne, Young Twickenham, Dan McCarthy and Jem Leonard all in 1815. In April the next year he beat George Dodd and Ikey Baruk, then in April 1817 knocked out "West Country Dick" at Moulsey Hurst, Surrey and followed this up by demolishing the highly rated Harry Holt in eight rounds.

Since Tom Belcher's retirement in 1813 and the defeat of Dutch Sam in 1814 by Bill Nosworthy, Jack Scroggins and Ned Turner had been touted by many as probably the two best middleweights around, but these results of Randall attracted the attention of the also highly rated middleweight Aby Belasco, who many recognized as the real successor to Dutch Sam and Tom Belcher. In September 1817 on Shepperton Range, Middlesex Randall and Belasco met, but after seven tough rounds lasting 55 minutes a thundering punch by Randall ended the fight which put paid to any pretensions Belasco might have had about being the best at this weight.

Randall then beat the formidable Joe Parish "The Waterman" in eleven rounds lasting 53 minutes on Hayes Common, Middlesex in November 1817, this fight giving Jack Randall general recognition as the best middleweight in the country and he then continued his winning ways over Philip Burke in 45 minutes on Wimbledon Common in June 1818. Randall then faced Dan McCarthy for a second time in a turn up, winning in 25 minutes at Drury Lane,

London and a rematch with Philip Burke ended with Randall thrashing Burke in twenty three rounds.

In December of the same year on Crawley Downs, Sussex, Randall met Ned Turner the highly rated middleweight, who had beaten the formidable Jack Scroggins and in a terrific contest lasting over two hours Randall eventually overcame Turner in thirty four rounds. This fight confirmed Jack Randall as undisputed king of the middleweights which quickly led to a challenge by yet another top rated fighter, Jack Martin, known as the "Master of the Rolls" through his trade as a baker. In a fight of epic proportions at Crawley Downs, Sussex in May 1819 Jack Martin was cut down to size in round nineteen by Randall, in a fight which lasted 45 minutes after which Martin was unable to answer the call of time.

Randall fought and beat Jem Hodd in four rounds five months later and then retired. However two years later with Jack Martin having beaten several top class fighters a tremendous amount of interest was aroused in the Nonpareil's comeback for another showdown with the baker. They met for the second time in September 1821 at Crawley Downs, Sussex where Jack Randall blasted Jack Martin into oblivion with a knockout in the first round to confirm his superiority at this weight.

Randall then retired for good, having never been beaten, the perfect 100% record, a record very few have attained. Always a drinker but no longer having to train for a fight his drinking increased and he died at the age of 33, yet another victim to succumb to the excesses of alcohol.

1808
Randall beat "Snuff" three times at the Archery Grounds.

1809
Jem Leonard, Bloomsbury Fields, London	W	5r.	45min.	

1810
Orie Henshaw, Marylebone, London	D		25min.	

1811
Jack Payne, Regents Park, London	W		20min.	

1812
Murphy, Irish labourer, St. Giles, London	W			

1815
Walton, Coombe Wood, London	W		10min.	5gns+purse

113

1816

George Dodd, Moulsey Hurst, Surrey	W		25min.	5gns+purse
Isaac Baruk, Coombe Wood, London	W	6r.	12min.	10gns+purse

1817

Dick West, Moulsey Hurst, Surrey	W	29r.	33min.	25gns.
Harry Holt, Coombe Wood, London	W	8r.	25min.	25 gns.
Aby Belasco, Shepperton Range, Middx.	W	7r.	54min.	50gns.

Now acclaimed as the best middleweight in the country.

Philip Burke, Westminster, London	W		13min.	£20
Joe Parish, Hayes Common, Middx.	W	11r.	53min.	200gns.

1818

Dan McCarthy, Drury Lane, London (turn-up)	W	15r.	25min.	
Philip Burke, Wimbledon Common, London	W	23r.	44min.	200gns.
Ned Turner, Crawley Hurst, Sussex	W	34r.	140min.	£200

1819

Jack Martin, Crawley Downs Sussex	W	19r.	49min.	£250
Jem Hood, Battersea Fields, London	W	4r.		

1821

Jack Martin, Crawley Downs, Sussex	W	1r.	8½min.	£600

After Jack Randall retired, claims for being the top middleweight between 1821-1828 vied between Ned Turner, Jack Martin, Pat Halton, Cy Davis, Barney Aaron, Bishop Sharpe and Alec Reid, with some claims more legitimate than others. However, although in the top rank of middleweights their reigns were either too brief, not generally recognized or the claims were not treated too seriously by the Fancy or the sporting press.

Aby Belasco
(Ring career 1816-1824)

Born: 1797   Died: Unknown

Aby Belasco was one of four brothers, all of whom joined the professional prize fighting ranks although he proved the most successful with his superior scientific talent, speed, agility and durability. He stood 5' 6½" tall and weighed in at around 147lbs.-150lbs. throughout his career in the prize ring and facing his first recorded opponent only known as "Cribb's Coalheaver" in 1816 and winning after 30 minutes, although no other details are known of this fight.

In early 1817 Belasco met the challenge of another young fighter who was to make his mark in the sport, namely Josh Hudson at Woolwich, London and after a tough battle lasting 90 minutes, due to a dispute the fight was stopped with the purse awarded to Belasco. Later that year at Moulsey Hurst, Surrey Aby Belasco came up against the experienced Jack Payne, who had not only lost to Josh Hudson the year before, but several years earlier had been touted as the top middleweight in the country. In a contest lasting sixteen rounds, again Aby Belasco came out the winner which now gained him recognition from the Fancy of the London Prize Ring. Irishman Tom Reynolds, who was making his début in the prize ring, was the Jewish fighter's next opponent when they also clashed at Moulsey Hurst, which resulted in Belasco's first defeat when he was beaten by Reynolds, supposedly submitting after sixty six titanic rounds.

Although this was his first defeat, Belasco was still highly rated, so much so by the Jewish fraternity that he was pitched in to oppose the great and unbeaten Jack Randall, considered by many as already the best middleweight in the land. In an epic contest held at Shepperton Range, Hertfordshire, in which Belasco was the heavier man, with so much skill and science displayed by both warriors, Aby Belasco had to finally bow to the slightly more superior skills of Jack Randall after seven rounds, lasting a lengthy 54 minutes.

Aby Belasco might have slipped down in the estimation of the Fancy a bit after this defeat and it was in 1818, seven months after his defeat by Randall that he next entered the ring against someone only known as the "Whitcomb Man" at Cheltenham, Gloucestershire, who he thrashed in 12 minutes, although as no other details are available this may have been a turn-up after the Cheltenham Races or a street fight. Three months later he faced the up and coming Cy Davis at Rickmansworth, Hertfordshire, losing to the Bristolian in nine rounds. He finished the year on a winning streak though when he met Joe Townsend at Coventry beating him in a fight that lasted 24 minutes.

There are no recorded fights for the Jewish pugilist in 1819 but he opened up his account in 1820 with a win against the tough and durable Phil Sampson from Birmingham, a man who was to become an almost constant adversary as they were to meet another three times in the next three years. The first time was at Potter's Street, near Harlow, Essex in a contest that ended in a draw after eleven rounds; however when they met a week later in a room fight at Martin Street in London, Belasco was the winner in a gloved fight of nine rounds. In another room fight at Norwich the Jewish fighter then demolished Josh Hudson for a second time, this time in thirty five rounds lasting 40 minutes. Before the year of 1820 was concluded he met Phil Sampson for a third time, in another gloved fight at Windmill Street, London where Sampson reversed the tables beating Belasco in twelve rounds.

Again there are no recorded details of any fights for Aby Belasco until 1823 when, in a fight that attracted a large crowd he was in the opposite corner of the ring that was also occupied by Birmingham's pride and joy, Arthur Matthewson. The lighter Matthewson was unbeaten in the three years that he had been active in the fistic world, which included 20 bye battles amongst his recorded 22 fights so far and he was a skilful, fast and strong battler. He was also too good for the Jewish man hammering him to defeat in fifteen rounds, lasting 44 minutes at Moulsey Hurst, Surrey to continue his unbeaten run of wins. A few weeks later, none the worse for wear it seems, the brave Belasco was back in the ring at Harpenden Common, Hertfordshire and back to winning ways with an eleven round win over Pat Halton who was dubbed the "Irish Champion", albeit with only two recorded fights before that, a draw and a win, although the draw was against the recognized Irish Champion, Jack Langan. Later that year Aby Belasco again faced his old adversary Phil Sampson at Crawley Downs, Sussex in what was now a grudge match, as after their third fight three years earlier Sampson apparently made some disparaging remarks about the Jewish race. Alas victory was not to be for Belasco

116

as he went down under the pounding fists of the bigger and heavier Phil Sampson after twenty five rounds. At least they resolved their differences after this fight and became firm friends.

In 1824 the indomitable Jew had one last fight against George Weston at Shepperton, Surrey which he easily won in three rounds. After he had retired from the ring he took on the role of a second in several fights, notably for his old foe, but now close friend, Phil Sampson, until he got into trouble with the law. Not long after that he sadly died although the exact date is not known.

1816

"Cribb's Coalheaver"	W		30 min.	5gns+purse

1817

Josh Hudson, Woolwich, London	W		90min.	10gns.
Jack Payne, Moulsey Hurst, Surrey	W	16r.	17min.	8gns.
Tom Reynolds, Moulsey Hurst, Surrey	L	66r.	80min.	20gns.
Jack Randall, Shepperton Range, Surrey	L	7r.	54min.	100gns.

1818

"Whitcomb Man", Cheltenham, Gloucs.	W		12min.	20gns.
Cy Davis, Rickmansworth, Herts.	L	9r.	10min.	20gns.
Joe Townsend, Coventry, Warks.	W		24min.	10gns.

1820

Phil Sampson, Potter's Street, Essex	D	11r.		50gns.
Phil Sampson, Martin Street, London (gloves)	W	9r.		
Josh Hudson, Norwich (room-fight)	W	35r.	40min.	£5
Phil Sampson, Windmill Street, London (gloves)	L	12r.		

1823

Arthur Matthewson, Moulsey Hurst, Surrey	L	15r.	44min.	£100
Pat Halton, Harpendon Common, Herts.	W	11r.	27min.	50gns.
Phil Sampson, Crawley Downs, Sussex	L	24r.	42min.	£100

1824

George Weston, Shepperton, Surrey	W	3r.	£16

Jack Martin
(Ring career 1816-1828)

Born: 1796   Died: 1868

"Master of the Rolls"

Born at Kennington, London, near the church, Jack Martin earned his non de plume "Master of the Rolls" from a young age through his calling as a baker, although participating in fights with other local lads in the area in his spare time. He stood 5' 9" tall and weighed 153-158lbs. during his fighting career and was described as scientific speedy, agile and two fisted and being one of many fine pugilists at middleweight around at that time.

His first recorded fight, in 1816, was against George Oliver, brother of the more famous Tom Oliver, at Ilford, Essex where he succeeded in being the victor after twenty one rounds. Two years later, Martin was matched against the well-known and successful Jack Johnson at Hale, Middlesex but Johnson was completely outclassed by the baker in just thirteen rounds and had to be carried out of the ring.

With the potential that the 22 year old Martin had shown in these two fights he was pitched in with top middleweight bruiser Jack Scroggins at Moulsey Hurst, Surrey at the end of 1818. In a fight where both men took severe punishment it was Jack Martin that emerged the winner after sixty five gruelling rounds. This success earned him the right to have a shot at Jack Randall, considered by most as the best middleweight in the land. They met at Crawley Downs, Sussex in 1819 and when Randall quickly found his range it was soon over for Martin as he was given a boxing lesson by the "Nonpareil" in nineteen rounds lasting just 49 minutes.

Top rated Ned Turner who had also been beaten by Jack Randall was now challenged by Jack Martin and the two met later in 1819 at Wallingham Common, Surrey. It emerged that Turner was too clever for Martin and resoundingly beat the baker in forty rounds of a pretty one sided fight, with the Fancy wondering if Jack Martin had maybe been pushed in too early in accepting fights against top class fighters.

Martin's next fight at the end of a bad year for him was a win in two rounds against Josh Hudson at Colnbrook, Buckinghamshire, when a powerful punch from Martin dislocated Hudson's shoulder and forced him to quit. At Farnham Royal, Buckinghamshire in 1820 Martin faced Jack Cabbage in a contest that lasted for seventy five rounds before he got the better of the lighter Jack "Strong Arm" Cabbage. Later that year he climbed into the ring with Phil Sampson and defeated him in twenty nine rounds, that were not a true reflection of his skills, as he mauled and pulled Sampson to defeat. In that same year, at Lewes Races in Sussex Martin was challenged by a gypsy, John Cooper who was possibly drunk and a small subscription was quickly raised as a purse. The gypsy, who turned out to be no real threat to the baker was badly beaten in ten rounds and sent on his way. This impromptu challenge did however attract the interest of the much acclaimed Dave Hudson, brother of Josh Hudson, who Martin had beaten the previous year. This contest was held at Moulsey Hurst, Surrey and Dave Hudson went the same way as his brother although he did last longer, with Jack Martin taking eighteen rounds to dispose of him.

Ned Turner was now challenged again by the baker and they met at Crawley, Sussex in 1821 and in a classic fight Jack Martin became the eventual winner after sixty epic rounds, after Turner, totally exhausted, was unable to rise from his second's knee. Martin was probably now considered the best middleweight in the land as the unbeaten Jack Randall had now retired. Randall was at ringside and now challenged Martin to meet him in the ring, with the challenge being immediately accepted by the Master of the Rolls. Three months after the Turner fight Jack Martin squared up to the now legendary Jack Randall in a ring at Crawley, Sussex to decide the best man at middleweight in the country. Jack Randall proved that he was, by sensationally pummelling Jack Martin to defeat in one round and before some of the crowd had even settled themselves down. With this win Randall retired for good.

The baker was prepared to carry on in his pursuit of ring glory; however several contests were forfeited for one reason or another throughout 1822-1824. He married and settled down to a life as an inn-keeper and gave up the idea of further ring battles and Jack Martin did not enter the lists again until, after an argument, he was challenged by another fighting legend, Young Dutch Sam. They faced each other at Knowle Hill, Berkshire in 1828 but a now 32 year old Jack Martin was no match for a great boxer such as Sam, 12 years his junior and in his prime. After seven one-sided rounds the baker was done for, being swept aside in just 16 minutes by the man known as the "Phenomenon". It was Jack Martin's last fight and after some years spent in the licensing trade he retired, first to St. Albans and then to the county of Devon, becoming a vegetarian and abstainer of alcohol and living until he was 75.

1816

George Oliver, Ilford, Essex	W	21r.	29min.	20gns.

1818

Jack Johnson,Hale, Middx.	W	13r.	30min.	100gns.
Jack Scroggins, Moulsey Hurst, Surrey	W	65r.	122min.	£200+purse

1819

Jack Randall,Crawley Downs, Sussex	L	19r.	49min.	£250
Ned Turner, Wallingham Common, Surrey	L	40r.	67min.	100gns.
Josh Hudson, Colnbrook, Bucks.	W	2r.	9min.	100gns.

1820

Jack Cabbage,Farnham Royal, Bucks.	W	75r.	72min.	200gns.
Phil Sampson, North Walsham, Norfolk	W	29r.		£100
John Cooper, Lewes Races, Sussex	W	10r.	17min.	£25+purse
David Hudson, MoulseyHurst, Surrey	W	18r.	39min.	

1821

Ned Turner, Crawley, Sussex	W	60r.	88min.	200gns.
Jack Randall, Crawley, Sussex	L	1r.	8min.	300gns.

1828

Young Dutch Sam, Knowle Hill, Berks .	L	7r.	16min.	£100

Bishop Sharpe
(Ring career 1817-1828)

Born: 1798   Died: 1861

"The Bold Smuggler"

Bishop Sharpe was born in Woolwich, London at the end of the 18th century and when he grew up he entered the Royal Navy, however as his nickname suggests he was, at times, at odds with His Majesty's Revenue Officers. Standing 5' 7" tall and weighing 154lbs. he was known to be a crude but strong bruiser who relied mostly on bull-like charges at his opponents and relying on swinging, powerful punches to win the day. Sharpe first turned to prize fighting in 1817, his opponent only known as the "Deptford Carrier" who he beat in fourteen rounds at Shooters Hill, London. The next year of 1818 saw Sharpe beat Jack Lester at Blackheath, London in forty eight rounds and Bob Hall at Woolwich in forty five rounds. Following these successes he beat Dick Prior at Woolwich Marshes in twenty five rounds and then John Street at Charlton, Kent in one hundred rounds in 1819. In 1820 further successes followed when he beat John King at Plumstead, London in twenty five rounds and Tom Cooper at Hampton Races also in twenty five rounds.

Fame for Bishop Sharpe was now growing in the capital and in 1822 he stepped up a class by taking on Phil Burke at Plumstead Marshes, London and beating him in forty nine rounds to further enhance his growing reputation with the London Prize Ring. He was now matched with tough and durable Gypsy Jack Cooper in Epping Forest, Essex in 1823 and after the first thirteen rounds the fight was pretty even, after that the gypsy seemed to be getting the better of his man, but the smuggler rallied and by round forty five he was the stronger man, finishing Cooper off in round fifty six. Two months later they met again at Harpenden Common, Hertfordshire where once again in a repeat of the first fight Bishop Sharpe overcame the gypsy in thirty six rounds this time. They met for a third time three months later at Blackheath, London where after twenty one rounds darkness beat them, so resulting in a drawn contest.

Alec Reid, also a Londoner and also making a name for himself with the London Prize Ring was next up for Sharpe in 1824, but in a shambolic fight in which Reid appeared lethargic and disinterested, the stakes were withdrawn after four rounds lasting just three minutes. Reid claimed afterwards that he was unwell but the general opinion at ringside was that it was probably a fixed fight.

In the next year of 1825 Sharpe was in a turn-up with Tom Cooper, a man he had beaten almost five years earlier, at the Old Barge House, Essex, but this time he had to be content with a draw after seventeen rounds. Ben Warwick was then articled to fight Sharpe and they faced each other at Chatham, London in which after twenty five rounds Bishop Sharpe was again the winner and still unbeaten. These winning ways carried on into 1826 when he clashed with Alec Reid once again, this time at No Man's Land, Hertfordshire, where although Reid was judged the better man overall, it was Sharpe with a powerful blow to the body in round sixteen that signalled the beginning of the end for Reid, the fight eventually ending in round twenty by which time Reid was unable to continue and Sharpe was declared the winner.

He was now considered a top middle weight and Tom Gaynor was Bishop Sharpe's next opponent at Sheremere, Bedfordshire and although Gaynor was taller and heavier he did not use it to its full effect in a fast and furious fight and Sharpe with his constant boring in tactics and throws eventually won the day after seventy rounds. In 1828 the Bold Smuggler and Alec Reid met once again at No Man's Land, Hertfordshire and in a classic contest Bishop Sharpe was beaten for the first and only time in the prize ring after a titanic ninety one rounds. After this fight an attempt to match him with Young Dutch Sam fell through and Sharpe fell into obscurity, appearing only in sparring benefits or as a second at minor fights and bye battles.

1817

The "Deptford Carrier", Shooters Hill, London	W	14r.	21min.	

1818

Jack Lester, Blackheath, London	W	48r.		
Bob Hall, Woolwich, London	W	45r.	5min.	£100

1819

Dick Prior, Woolwich Marshes, London	W	25r.	35min.	£50
John Street, Charlton, Kent	W	100r.	105min.	£50

1820

John King, Plumstead, London	W	25r.	40min.	£50
Tom Cooper, Hampton Races	W	25r.	40min.	£10

1822

Phil Burke, Plumstead Marshes, London	W	49r.	64min.	30gns.

1823

Gypsy Jack Cooper, Epping Forest, Essex	W	56r.	85min.	£100
Gypsy Jack Cooper, Harpenden Common, Herts.	W	36r.	39min.	£100
Gypsy Jack Cooper, Blackheath, London	D	21r.	24min.	£100

1824

Alec Reid, Moulsey Hurst, Surrey (fixed fight?)	D	4r.	3min.	£100

1825

Tom Cooper, Old Barge House, Essex (turn-up)	D	17r.		
Ben Warwick,Chatham, London	W	25r.		£25

1826

Alec Reid, No Man's Land, Herts.	W	20r.	24min.	£100
Tom Gaynor, Sheremere, Beds.	W	70r.	78min.	£100

1828

Alec Reid, No Man's Land, Herts	L	91r.	87min.	£100

Alec Reid
(Ring career 1820-1830)

Born: 1802   Died: 1876

"The Chelsea Snob"

Alec Reid was born in Guernsey, in the Channel Islands, his father being in the British Army and after being invalided out took up residence in Chelsea Barracks with the now 14 year old Alec being apprenticed to a shoemaker or "snob", and hence he was known as the "Chelsea Snob". Young Alec Reid grew up to be 5' 7" in height and weighed around 147lbs. and after honing his pugilistic skills around London, he turned out to be a very clever boxer who combined speed, strength and agility.

His first recorded fight in 1820 was against a heavier and taller man called Finch at Five Fields, Belgravia, London, who Reid disposed of in two rounds and then again in five rounds at Chelsea, London in 1821. Alec Reid got off to a winning start with his first opponent in 1822, defeating Sam Abbott at Wimbledon Common, London, followed by wins against someone only known as the "Walham Green Snob" at Moulsey Hurst, Surrey and finally Jem Hearns at the same venue. 1823 was a busy year for Reid when taking on and beating Bob Yandall at Battersea Fields, London and Paddy O'Rafferty at Hampton Common, London before suffering the first defeat of his career when facing the useful Dick Defoe in Epping Forest, where he was beaten in thirteen rounds. He returned to winning ways, firstly against someone only known as the "Brompton Brickmaker" on Crawley Downs, Sussex, then against a waterman called Tom Harris in fourteen rounds at Moulsey Hurst, Surrey and rounded off the year with a another win when defeating Joe Underhill at Chatham Lines, London, when Underhill could take no further punishment after eight rounds.

After Pearce Inglis defeated Ned Turner at Colnbrook, Buckinghamshire in 1824 the following bout was Alec Reid against Gypsy John Cooper. In a fight that was fought at a frantic pace, especially by the gypsy, Reid had to be on his guard all the time as Cooper turned up the heat from the start of the contest and up until about round fifteen many of the crowd thought that Cooper would win out in the end; however the calmer and more controlled hitting power of Reid finally won the day in round nineteen.

Later in the year and returning from watching the prize fight between Harry Jones losing to Ned Stockman in Epping Forest, an altercation arose between Reid and the bigger Maurice Delap, although Reid apparently held his own for a couple of rounds before they were parted; however about 30 minutes later Bill Savage also challenged Reid near Temple Mills, Essex for a subscription purse quickly gathered by the spectators present and after five rounds the impromptu turn-up was declared a draw as darkness closed in and the purse was shared.

Reid was now matched with highly rated Bishop Sharpe, unbeaten in eleven recorded contests and a tough customer, but with only little boxing science or skill. They met in 1824 at Moulsey Hurst in a fight that only lasted four rounds and three minutes of fighting, as Reid went down rather tamely claiming that he felt unwell. Stakes were drawn and although the contest was declared a draw many people suspected the fight was fixed, but it was never proved. In March 1826 Reid beat Dick Price at Woodstock, Oxfordshire in nine rounds, a fight which may have been a turn-up with no other details of the contest. Later that year a fight was fixed against Matthew Jubb, billed as the "Cheltenham Champion" at Icombe near Stow-on-the-Wold, Gloucestershire. Jubb had also beaten Dick Price who was billed at the time as the "Oxford Champion". Although the acclaimed champion of Cheltenham put up a brave fight Alec Reid was the better man throughout, finally seeing off his man in eighteen rounds.

Tom Gaynor was Alec Reid's next opponent when they faced each other At No Man's Land, Hertfordshire in 1826 and in an epic fight the brave Reid finally conceded defeat to the Bath carpenter after thirty four rounds, only the second defeat of his career. Time was now ripe for Alec Reid and Bishop Sharpe to square up to each other again and so it was arranged for them to meet in No Man's Land, with Sharpe beating the Chelsea Snob in twenty rounds, although Reid was robbed of victory when within his grasp. A return contest was fixed for the next year, once again at No Man's Land and this time Reid was victorious in a brutal battle that raged for ninety one rounds before he was able to quell Bishop Sharpe's wild and dangerous lunges and crude attacks.

Ever since Dick Curtis from London was surprisingly beaten by the Oxfordshire born Jack Perkins in 1828 the London Prize Ring wanted a good, strong Londoner to beat the country bumpkin that had brought down their favourite pugilist. Alec Reid seemed to fit the bill and in 1830 articles were then signed for Reid and Perkins to meet at a venue where four counties met, Berkshire, Oxfordshire, Warwickshire and Worcestershire, called Four-shirestone to avoid interruption from the law. Described at the time as a classic fight where Alec Reid suffered heavy punishment before obtaining victory after fifty four rounds, it has to also be recognized that Jack Perkins went down to a brave and glorious defeat with the result still in doubt up until round fifty.

This was the last time Alec Reid appeared in the ring, now suffering from several injuries from his ring wars that he had taken part in he used his knowledge and experience at exhibitions and as a successful teacher of the sport. After that he also worked at Nat Langham's establishment, dying in relative poverty and obscurity at the ripe old age of 73.

1820

Finch	W	2r.	10min.	

1821

Finch, Five Fields, Chelsea, London	W	5r.	10min.	

1822

Sam Abbott,Wimbledon Common, London	W		25min.	Purse
Walham Green Snob, Moulsey Hurst, Surrey	W		10min.	
Jem Hearns, Moulsey Hurst, Surrey	W		15min.	25gns+purse

1823

Bob Yandall,Battersea Fields, London	W		90mins	.£10
Paddy O'Rafferty,Hampton Common, London	W	31r.	63min.	£9
Dick Defoe, Epping Forest, Essex	L	13r.	9min.	£30
"Brompton Brickmaker" Crawley Downs, Sussex	W		45min.	Purse
Tom Harris, Moulsey Hurst, Surrey	W	14r.	15min.	£20
Joe Underhill, Chatham Lines, London	W	8r.	19min.	25gns+purse

1824

Gypsy Jack Cooper, Colnbrook, Bucks.	W	19r.	29min.	£20+purse
Bill Savage,Temple Mills, Essex *(turn up)*	D		37min.	£5+purse
Bishop Sharpe, Moulsey Hurst, Surrey (fixed fight?)	D	4r.	3min.	£100

1825

Dick Price, Woodstock, Oxon.	W	9r.		Purse
Matthew Jubb, Icomb, Glouc.	W	18r.	24min.	£200

1826

Tom Gaynor, No Man's Land, Herts.	L	34r.	70min.	£100
Bishop Sharpe, No Man's Land, Herts	L	20r.	24min.	£100

1828

Bishop Sharpe, No Man's Land, Herts.	W	91r.	87min.	£100

1830

Jack Perkins, Four-shirestone	W	54r.	60min.	£200

Tom Gaynor
(Ring career 1821-1834)

Born: 1799 Died: 1834

"The Bath Carpenter"

Born in Bath, in the then county of Somerset and the son of a carpenter, it was reputed that Tom, as a boy, idolized an uncle of his who was apparently acclaimed as the Champion of Somerset and it was him that taught the young Tom the rudiments of boxing. Apprenticed as a carpenter at 13 years old in Taunton, it was during this time that Tom honed his fighting skills against other local youths with a certain fiddler by the name of Tom Turle, who found out to his detriment when challenging him and getting a pasting for his trouble. Other fights and turn-ups, brief in their description show no other details apart from the fact that Tom won them all.

Tom Gaynor stood 5' 10½" and weighed around 160lbs. which bordered on the roughly defined heavyweight and middleweight classes. Gaynor was considered to be a skilful fighter with great speed, strength and durability. In 1824 with his sights set on travelling to London, he lodged at the public house of the respected boxer Harry Holt and after arriving he fought an exhibition with gloves against the highly rated Josh Hudson. Because of his good showing Gaynor was pitched in with highly rated 168lb. heavyweight Ned Neale later that year at Shepperton Range, Surrey and although he lost, young Tom went down fighting bravely in twenty one rounds. A year later at Epsom Races he volunteered to enter the ring with Jonathan Bissell, known as "Young Gas", although being out of condition, while Bissell was in top shape and this soon told when after thirty one rounds Tom Gaynor was again beaten.

In 1826 Gaynor signed articles to take on the top class Alec Reid, known as the "Chelsea Snob" who had lost only once in sixteen previous battles. They met at No Man's Land, Hertfordshire in what turned out to be a terrific fight with both men giving their all, but in the end proved successful for the Bath carpenter when Reid was rendered insensible after thirty four rounds. Bishop Sharpe known as "The Bold Smuggler" was his next opponent, at Sheremere, Bedfordshire in which, after a hard and brutal fight lasting seventy

128

eight rounds, Tom Gaynor gave his all, but to no avail, as Sharpe proved too good for him on the day. He did not fight again until 1828 when he took on the only average rated Charles Gybletts, although noted as quite a scientific fighter. They also met at Sheremere, the venue of Gaynor's previous fight and in a contest that was a credit to both men it was Gybletts that could not answer the call to come to scratch for round fifty two and so Gaynor was declared the winner.

The Bath carpenter apparently did not fight again for three years during which time he enjoyed life as a publican, until he signed up to meet his old adversary of seven years previously, Ned Neale "The Streatham Youth". They faced each other at Warfield, Berkshire in 1831 and after a cautious start by both men Gaynor started to take control, but Neale then had the better of the next few rounds. After round thirty six Neale's stamina seemed to fall away, which may have been due to his punishing loss to Young Dutch Sam just a couple of months earlier and the popular Tom Gaynor ran out the eventual winner after forty five rounds.

Tom Gaynor was now 31 years of age and after returning to his trade as publican maybe he was resigned to the fact that he had fought his last battle in the prize ring, but after a couple of years out of the ring he was challenged by the unbeaten Young Dutch Sam, a man eight years younger, to enter the lists with him. Not to duck a challenge Gaynor faced the unbeaten Sam at Andover, Wiltshire in 1834, where the now veteran carpenter put in a fantastic display of guts and bravery, considering the disadvantage he was under with age and fitness, only going down under the blazing fists of his formidable younger opponent after over two hours of fierce fighting which took in just seventeen rounds. It was not only Tom Gaynor's last fight, but Young Dutch Sam's as well. Five months later the Bath carpenter was dead, due apparently to a chronic disease of several years standing.

1821

| Wescott | W |
| Wescott | W |

1822

| Wescott | W |
| George Mellish | W |

1823

| Tom Turle | W |
| Bill Hersey | W |

1824
Ned Neale, Shepperton Range, Surrey   L   21r.   70min.   £100

1825
Jonathan Bissell, Epsom Downs, Surrey   L   31r.   85min.   50gns.

1826
Alec Reid, No Man's Land, Herts.   W   34r.   70min.   £100
Bishop Sharpe, Sheremere, Beds.   L   78r.   70min.   £10

1828
Charles Gybletts, Sheremere, Beds.   W   51r.   113min.   £100

1831
Ned Neale, Warfield, Berks   W   45r.   111min.   £500

1834
Young Dutch Sam, Andover, Wilts.   L   17r.   125min.   £500

Harry Jones
(Ring career 1821-1834)

Born: 1804   Died: 1835

"Sailor Boy"

Born in Bristol which had a large sea port, Harry
Jones went to sea from an early age before
giving up the seafaring life to try his luck in the prize ring, after
probably learning how to use his fists on board ship. Only 5' 5" in
height and weighing around 140lbs.-144lbs. Jones was an
exceptionally strong, tough pugilist but a crude bruiser with little
skill, although he knew no fear and would mix it with anyone, which
helped gain him reasonable success over the years as a prize fighter.

His début in the sport did not start too well, in his first fight in 1821
against Luke Latham at Moulsey Hurst, Surrey he lost in thirty six
rounds and his second fight in 1822 against Ned Stockman at
Rutledge Common, London also resulted in a loss. Six months later
he faced Stockman again at Moulsey Hurst, Surrey but this time Jones
sprained an ankle in the first round and was unable to continue. 1823
saw his first success in the ring when he beat Charles Watts at
Primrose Hill, London and he was also successful against Bill Riley
at the same venue, but Jones then suffered another loss against Peter
Brookery. 1824 was a busy year for Harry Jones, after a turn up with
Ned Brown he defeated Jem Aldridge (on the same day as he got
married), lost to the much heavier Dick Price, an Oxford butcher, lost
to Tom Reidie and then lost again to Ned Stockman. He then beat
Frederick Edwards, a coachman and then finished off the year with a
win over Mick Curtain, all these fights being around the London area
apart from the contest with Dick Price which was near Oxford.

At this point in his career Jones was only winning most of his fights
against poor opposition, against stiffer antagonists he was getting
beaten and 1825 started in the same vein with a win over a certain
"Captain" Corduroy at The Barge House, Woolwich, London, but a
convincing win against a tough local who was acclaimed as the
Westminster Champion, Tommy O'Lynn in five rounds at Old Oak
Common, London sent Jones reputation with the Fancy spiralling.
Because of this he was matched against the new marvel Young Dutch

Sam, who was unbeaten after two previous fights in which he had shown prominent signs of his increasing and awesome talent. They met at Sheremere, Bedfordshire and in a fight that lasted eighteen rounds before Sam got the better of him; Harry Jones put a terrific fight and was the better man for most of the fight. As a result of this fight Jones was now in popular demand as 1826 showed, when winning against Jack Nolan at No Man's Land, Hertfordshire in seven rounds, Mick Curtain at St. Albans, Hertfordshire in 30 minutes, Tom Collins at Grays, Essex in four rounds, George Pick the "Bristol Youth" at No Man's Land, Hertfordshire in twenty seven rounds and finally Reuben Howe at Newmarket, Norfolk in thirty one rounds.

The Fancy were now taking a very keen interest in Harry Jones with the result that in 1827 the quality of his opponents improved and the purses increased. At Royston Heath, Cambridge he was up against Charles Gybletts, but was outclassed in 10 minutes, however two months later at Ickleton, Cheshire he took on the clever Jem Raines but after round three the contest was stopped by police and a draw declared. Bob Simmonds, a chimney sweep by trade was Jones next opponent at Bulpham Fen, Essex, a fight won easily by Jones in seventeen rounds. A second fight with Jem Raines was arranged and came off near Watford, Hertfordshire but although Raines countered well at times the ex-sailor fought bravely to overcome his opponent after twenty two rounds. Ike Dodd next threw his hat in the ring against Jones at Westbourne Common, Sussex and took a terrible beating for eighteen rounds before he was defeated.

The year of 1828 now saw Harry Jones in with premier pugilists and first up was Bill Savage at Chertsey, London and in a battle in which Savage never gave up, Harry Jones was his superior throughout, although it took fifty six rounds to quieten him. The now highly rated Ned Stockman who he had fought three times in previous years and never beaten was his next opponent, but this time he was the winner over Stockman in forty three rounds. The charismatic and top class Barney Aaron who had lost an epic fight to the great lightweight Dick Curtis the previous year was chosen as Harry Jones next opponent. Having gained weight Aaron and Jones weighed about the same when they threw their hats into the ring at The Barge House, Woolwich, London but in eighteen rounds of sharp fighting it was Jones who came out the winner. Tom Reidie, another previous opponent who had beaten him was next on the list but had the tables reversed when he was done for after sixteen rounds at Hurley Bottom, Berkshire.

With these successes Harry Jones was now considered in the top echelon of middleweights in the country with Young Dutch Sam being generally recognized as the number one. In 1829 Jones took on the useful Frank Redmond at No Man's Land, Hertfordshire, winning in ten rounds, followed two months later by George Watson at Harpenden Common, Hertfordshire who was beaten in thirty rounds. Taking 1830 off from pugilism Jones returned in 1831 to beat Dick Hill (the Nottingham Champion) at Bagthorpe Common, Nottinghamshire in a titanic struggle, but overcoming him in sixty nine rounds. Jack Perkins famous for his defeat of the unfit and until then unbeaten great Dick Curtis, rated by most as the greatest ever of the lightweights, was the ex-sailor's next opponent. Perkins was quite a bit heavier than Curtis and over the lightweight limit and so it was not considered as a fight for Curtis's accolade. Perkins was also generally recognized as overrated anyway and would probably have not lived with Curtis at his best. When he met Jones at Hurley Bottom, Berkshire in 1832 he was well beaten in twenty two rounds and so ended any pretensions Perkins had of gaining lasting fame.

Now suffering chronic lung disease Harry Jones next took on Gypsy Jack Cooper at Chertsey, London in 1833 and although both men took heavy punishment it was a long drawn out affair in which Jones was the eventual winner after twenty six rounds lasting over two hours. In his last fight in 1834 against Tom Smith at Shrubs Hill, Buckinghamshire, it was a very ill and tired Harry Jones who surrendered after just five rounds of fighting. In 1835 after being admitted to hospital again with lung problems, "Sailor Boy" Harry Jones died at the age of 35.

1821

Luke Latham, Moulsey Hurst, Surrey	L	26r.	33min.	8gns.

1822

Ned Stockman, Rutledge Common, London	L	38r.	40min.	£5+purse
Ned Stockman, Moulsey Hurst, Surrey	L	1r.		

(Jones sprained his ankle and unable to continue-subscription purse divided)

1823

Charlie Watts, Primrose Hill, London	W	23min.	£10
Bill Riley, Primrose Hill, London	W	30min.	£10
Peter Brookery, Primrose Hill, London	L	45min.	

1824

Ned Brown, Paddington, London (turn-up)	W	19r.	33min.	£15+purse
Jem Aldridge	W		12min.	£10
Dick Price, Picksey Meadow, Oxford	L	15r.	21min.	
Tom Reidie, Battersea Park, London	L		165min.	
Ned Stockman, Epping Forest, Essex	L	17r.	23min.	£50
Frederick Edwards, *unknown venue*	W		90min.	purse
Mick Curtain, Battersea Fields, London	W		75min.	

1825

Captain Corduroy, Old Barge House, London	W	21r.	20min.	
Tom O'Lynn, Old Oak Common, London	W	5r.	6min.	£5+purse
Young Dutch Sam, Sheremere, Beds.	L	18r.	53min.	£50

1826

Jack Nolan, No Man's Land, Herts.	W	7r.	15min.	£5+purse
Mick Curtain, St. Albans, Herts.	W		30min.	£5
Tom Collins, Grays, Essex	W	4r.	6min.	£5
George Pick, No Man's Land, Herts.	W	27r.	30min.	£5
Reuben Howe, Newmarket, Suffolk	W	31r.	34min.	£5

1827

Charles Gibletts, Royston Heath, Cambs.	L		10min.	purse
Jem Raines, Ickleton, Essex	D	3r.		£50
(stopped by police)				
Bob Simmonds, Bulphan Fen, Essex	W	17r.	35min.	
Jem Raines, Watford, Herts.	W	22r.	95min.	£50
Ike Dodd, Westbourne Common, London	W	18r.	34min.	£20+purse

1828

Bill Savage, Chertsey, London	W	56r.	95min.	£50
Ned Stockman, Sheremere, Beds.	W	43r.		£50
Barney Aaron, Old Barge House, London	W	18r.	15min.	£100
Tom Reidie, Hurley Bottom, Berks.	W	16r.	22min.	£60

1829

Frank Redmond, No Man's Land, Herts.	W	10r.	36min.	£200
George Watson, Harpenden Common, Herts.	W	30r.	39min.	£100

1831

Dick Hill, Bagthorpe Common, Notts.	W	69r.	80min.	£200

1832

Jack Perkins, Hurley Bottom, Berks.	W	22r.	46min.	£100

1833

Gypsy Jack Cooper, Chertsey, London	W	26r.	130min.	£50

1834

Tom Smith, Shrubs Hill, Bucks.	L	5r.	14min.	£100

Young Dutch Sam
(Acclaimed as the best in the land at a middle weight 1827-1834)

Born: 1808   Died: 1843

"The Phenomenon"

Young Dutch Sam (real name Samuel Evans) was another of the greatest bare knuckle fighters that England ever produced, not surprising as he was the son of the immortal "Dutch Sam" who was considered by many as the greatest pound for pound pugilist of the bareknuckle era. He was apprenticed to a local printer in London as a youngster and was involved in the usual scraps that many boys got involved in at that age, probably winning them all.

Since the retirement of the incomparable Jack Randall in 1821 the void that appeared in the middleweight scene was partly filled by several very good fighters, but although they might have considered themselves as the best or assumed the accolade, they were never really considered by the majority of the Fancy as truly the best, or better than any other. Others unfortunately suffered from being in the wrong place at the wrong time, especially around the late 1820's as Young Dutch Sam rose to prominence and ruled supreme in this division for several years. He stood a little less than 5' 9" and weighed from 144lbs.-154lbs.

Sam had his first paid fight at 17 years old when he outclassed Ned Stockman in July 1825 for a purse of £20. He often fought men much heavier, but because of his extraordinary skill, speed and punching power he was never defeated in any of his sixteen recorded contests, with his backer and patron, Mr. Hughes Ball never knowing what it was to lose a wager on him.

Sam is reputed to have beaten a man called Gypsy Tom Cooper in April 1826 at Grays, Essex, using only his left hand, with his right hand kept behind his back, whether he had hurt it hitting Cooper or was just supremely confident we shall never know! He beat Harry Jones "The Sailor Boy" in October 1825 at Sheremere, Bedfordshire and then Bill Carroll in June 1826 after the Ascot race meeting. In

1827, Jack Cooper "The Slashing Gypsy" at Andover, Hampshire and Dick Davies "The Pet of Manchester" at Haversham near Milton Keynes in February and June respectively went the same way as all Sam's previous opponents. The fight with Dick Davis lasted over a marathon three and a half hours in which just thirty rounds were fought and Sam was now considered the best at middleweight in the land. In October of that year Sam was supposed to have fought Bishop Sharpe but was arrested just before the fight and charged with a breach of the peace. He fought and beat veteran Jack Martin at Knowle Hill, Twyford, Berkshire in November 1828 in seven rounds which now consolidated his position as the best middleweight in the land. Ned Neale, in April 1829 at Ludlow, Shropshire was defeated in a seventy eight round epic fight and Neale was again beaten comprehensively again in January 1831, this time in fourteen rounds. In 1833 Sam was supposed to have fought Harry Preston, but he was arrested and bound over to keep the peace, because of his social life outside the ring. The next opponent for Sam was Tom Gaynor "The Bath Carpenter" who, when they met, had no answer to the pounding fists, speed and silky skills of his illustrious opponent and was beaten in seventeen rounds near Andover in June 1834.

Dutch Sam's downfall, like so many before and after him, was his lifestyle outside the ring which occasionally brought him into conflict with the law, culminating in 1838 when he was arrested and then bailed, when acting as a second for his friend, another great fighter, the lightweight Owen Swift. Swift was involved in a prize fight in which his opponent Bill Phelps died. Fleeing to France, Sam was arrested in Paris and sentenced to thirteen months in jail after taking part in an illegal sparring session with Swift. On his return to England he was arrested for his part in the Swift verses Phelps fight, tried, but found not guilty by the jury. An earlier offence in that same year when Sam, probably drunk, assaulted and flattened a police officer in a scuffle in the Royal Standard pub, Piccadilly had him arrested again, serving three months in jail as a guest of his Majesty the King.

After marrying a publican's daughter he took over the Black Lion in Vinegar Yard, Drury Lane, London and then the Old Drury Tavern in Brydges Street, Covent Garden, London. His health was by now gradually deteriorating, probably due to his lifestyle and he died of tuberculosis in November 1843 and buried in his wife's family vault at Kensal Green, London.

1823

Bill Dean, Kennington Common, London	W		45min.	

1825

Ned Stockman, Knowle Hill, Twyford, Berks.	W	17r.	36min.	£25
Harry Jones, Sheremere, Beds.	W	18r.	53min.	£50

1826

Tom Cooper, Grays, Essex	W	15r.	38min.	£60
Bill Carroll, Ascot Heath Races, Berks.	W	16r.	30min.	£50

1827

Gypsy Jack Cooper, Andover, Hants.	W	9r.	63min.	£100
Dick Davis, Haversham, Milton Keynes	W	30r.	215min.	£200

Now acclaimed as the best middleweight in the country.

1828

Jack Martin, Knowle Hill, Twyford, Berks.	W	7r.	16min.	£200

1829

Ned Neale, Ludlow, Shropshire	W	78r.	101min.	£20

1831

Ned Neale, Bumstead,	W	14r.	52min.	£420

1834

Tom Gaynor, Andover, Hampshire	W	17r.	125min.	£500

Again a vacuum in the middleweight division was left when Young Dutch Sam's glorious career in the prize ring came to a close, the only prominent middleweights around were probably Harry Preston and "Tass" Parker, until Johnny "Hammer" Lane appeared on the scene.

Johnny Lane
(Acclaimed as the best in the land at a middle weight 1836-1841)

Born: 1815   Died: 1865

"Hammer Lane"

Johnny Lane was born in Birmingham into a fighting family, as four of his brothers also followed him into the prize ring. He got the nickname of "Hammer" through his trade as a blacksmith and his all action style of fighting, helped by carrying a tremendous punch in either hand. This was also coupled with great speed and although lacking in any great boxing skill, no one doubted his courage. Well built, Lane stood 5' 8" and his weight varied as his career progressed from 135lbs.-150lbs.

His first recorded fight was against a certain Moses Sidaway at Plants Green, Birmingham in 1831, which he won in 12 minutes; this was followed up the next year with another win against Harry Ball in twenty one rounds at Smethwick, Birmingham. In November 1833 Lane came up against Bill Hewson and again was the victor in twenty sevenrounds, then after defeating Jack Green at Shirley, Birmingham in March 1835, Johnny Lane fought Tass Parker at Kensal Corner, London in a fight where Parker's hit and run tactics were no match for the raw power of Lane and after forty eight rounds Parker was done for.

Owen Swift, the man rated by the Fancy and sporting press as the king of the lightweights moved up in weight to challenge middleweight Hammer Lane and although Swift was over 14lbs. lighter than his opponent, it took Lane one hundred and four terrific rounds to subdue the gallant little lightweight star, at Four-shirestone in Warwickshire in 1836. The highly rated Jack Adams was the Hammer's next opponent when they met at Woodstock, Oxfordshire in August 1836 and although Lane was the winner, the manner in which he achieved victory, by head butting his opponent, forcing him to retire three rounds later, rather soured the occasion. Hammer Lane was now considered the premier middleweight in the country and in March 1837 he again met his fellow Brummie, Tass Parker in what turned out to be a repetition of their previous meeting two years earlier, however it took ninety six rounds to subdue Parker this time. Hammer Lane next took on Byng Stocks at Bicester, Oxfordshire in June 1838 and won in ten rounds, but his main danger and rival now was James Wharton, commonly known as "Young Molineaux", a top fighter who had worked his way up the ranks and was now ready to challenge Hammer Lane's claim as the best middleweight in the land. It was the clash of the top two middleweights in the country, both unbeaten after several years of fighting. In a fight of epic proportions at Linderick Common, Nottinghamshire in June 1840, fifty two magnificent rounds were contested, with the fight ebbing and flowing, firstly to Lane and then to Young Molineaux, but it was Molineaux who finally won the day and the acclamation of being claimed the best in the land at that weight.

It was Young Molineaux's last fight though and after an illustrious career, he retired immediately afterwards, however Lane lost his next fight to Yankee Sullivan seven months later in nineteen rounds, although the loss was probably due to the fact that he broke a bone in his right arm, in about round three and after a brave rearguard action for many more rounds, his seconds withdrew him from the fight, as he was so weak by then and unable to defend himself. Yankee Sullivan came out of the fight with little credit, as knowing Lane's arm was badly damaged he went for it most of the time which antagonized the crowd, especially Lane's supporters. With this loss he retired, but returned to the prize ring nine years later in June 1850 to take on Tom Davis, eventually losing in forty rounds.

At 48 years old Hammer Lane fought his last fight, when at Kingswood Common, Shropshire he fought a thirty four round draw with Jack Grant. Just over a year later the great and brave Hammer Lane was dead.

1831

Moses Sidaway, Plants Green, Birmingham	W		12min.	£10

1832

Harry Ball, Smethwick, Birmingham	W	21r.	35min.	£40

1833

Bill Hewson, Smethwick, Birmingham	W	27r.		£20

1835

Jack Green, Shirley, nr. Birmingham	W	23r.	38min.	£50
Tass Parker, Kensal Corner, London	W	48r.		£50

1836

Owen Swift, Four-shirestone, Warks.	W	104r.	123min.	£100
Jack Adams, Woodstock, Oxon.	W	16r.	42min.	£100

Now acclaimed as the best middleweight in the country.

1837

Tass Parker, Woodstock, Oxon.	W	96r.	120min.	£100

1838

Byng Stocks, Bicester, Oxon.	W	10r.	22min.	£200

1840

Young Molineaux, Linderick Common, Notts.	L	52r.	72min.	£200

1841

Yankee Sullivan, Linderick Common Notts.	L	19r.	34min.	£100

1850

Tom Davis, No Mans Land, Herts.	L	40r.	67min.	£100

1864

Jack Grant, Kingswood Common, Shropshire	D	34r.	50min.	£20

Tass Parker and Yankee Sullivan put in claims for the title that were not generally accepted by the Fancy or sporting press as legitimate claims, especially with Sullivan because after he beat Lane he returned to America.

James Wharton
(Acclaimed as the best in the land at a middle weight 1840)

Born: 1813   Died: 1856

"Young Molyneaux"

After Young Dutch Sam had retired he again had left a vacuum that was hard to fill, with various fighters, notably Tass Parker, Tom Britton and Harry Preston vying to be recognized as the best middleweight in the country, but failing to convince the Fancy that any of them in particular was so outstanding as to be called a true champion until "Hammer" Lane and James Wharton appeared on the scene.

Born in Tangier, Morocco, North Africa, James Wharton stood about 5' 8" tall and weighed around 154lbs. He worked as a steward for the East India Company and showed great promise as a fighter onboard ship and when the boat docked in London he was introduced to pugilist Jem Burn at his pub the Queens Head in The Haymarket, London. His first contest in April 1833 was against the tough Tom McKeever at Whetstone, Leicestershire and Wharton won in 38 rounds taking 54 minutes. He then went on to beat a man known as "The Hertfordshire Pippin" (George Evans) in eleven rounds and followed tis up with a win against Jack Wilsden at Colney Heath, Hertfordshire in thirteen rounds.

Running out of good eleven stoners around the London area Wharton ventured north and took on the experienced Bill Fisher in November 1835 at Woore, Shropshire and who he duly battered to defeat in forty nine rounds. He then fought Tom Britton in February 1836 at Buerton, Cheshire, in a titanic struggle of two hundred and one rounds lasting just over four hours. There was controversy in round s when Britton threw Wharton on to the ropes and continued to hit his entangled opponent. The umpires disagreed to the legality of these tactics with several of Britton's supporters, armed with bludgeons, harassing Wharton's seconds. The fight continued but in a ring with the ropes and stakes trampled and with very little room to manoeuvre as the crowd closed in. Both men eventually agreed to a draw when darkness fell.

In April 1837 at Woore, Shropshire, Wharton met the top rated and unbeaten Harry Preston who had defeated the experienced Tass Parker. Over ten thousand spectators turned up for this fight and after a quiet first round the pace quickened and after Wharton had thrown Preston in round thirteen, Preston began to tire. It was round sixteen and the last which was the most spectacular though, as again Wharton threw Preston who ended up entangled and upside down on the ropes, with his head doubled up under him. Fearing he could have broken his neck several people rushed to help release him and he was carried to his quarters at The Falcon Inn, Woore. Luckily all he suffered apart from concussion was a broken rib and so the man nicknamed "Young Molineaux" was now rated as the top middleweight in the country by the Fancy.

James Wharton then went on to beat the durable William Renwick, the Newcastle champion, at Cambo near Newcastle in October 1837 and after this fight Wharton decided to settle in the North, in Liverpool. In this area of the country he became very popular, being very much in demand with his sparring exhibitions and as a trainer and teacher, as well as a pugilist.

Hammer Lane from Birmingham was fast becoming a rising star in the Midlands and recognized by his supporters and many more from that area, as the best in the country when he pummeled the highly rated Jack Adams to defeat in 1836 at Woodstock, Oxfordshire, followed by Tass Parker at the same venue in 1837 and then Byng Stocks in ten rounds, lasting only 20 minutes at Bicester, Oxfordshire in 1838. Efforts were made to bring Wharton and Lane together as they were now rated as easily the two best middleweight men around at this time, beating all the top men between them. Meanwhile in March 1839 a rematch with William Renwick proved just as tough for Wharton as the first fight, taking him sixty four rounds to dispose of Renwick.

In June 1840 the fight everyone wanted to see, James Wharton facing up against Hammer Lane, took place at Lindwick Common, near Sheffield and from the outset it became the epic that was expected between these two fine gladiators, both declaring they would retire after the fight. The opening rounds were about even, then Lane began to get the better of the exchanges until, in the twenty

142

second round, a pile driver almost finished Lane and from then on it was all Wharton until he eventually knocked Lane cold in round fifty two. Hammer Lane did come out of retirement about six months later when he fought English born American Yankee Sullivan where he had to eventually succumb in round nineteen after breaking his arm in the third round!

With this victory over Hammer Lane, Wharton or Young Molyneaux as he was commonly known retired as he promised and so ended up undefeated. By the time he was 40 years old he was suffering from consumption, dying three years later in poverty in Liverpool at the age of 43.

1833
Tom McKeever, Whetstone, Leics.	W	38r.	54min.	£10

1834
George Evans, Greenstreet Green, Kent	W	11r.		£10

1835
Jack Wilsden, Colney Heath, Herts.	W	13r.	22min.	£20
Bill Fisher, Woore, Cheshire	W	49r.	70min.	£48

1836
Tom Britton, Burton, Cheshire	D	201r.	247min.	£100

1837
Harry Preston, Woore, Cheshire	W	16r.	61min.	£200

Now acclaimed as the best middleweight in the country.

Will Renwick, Middleton Ridge, Newcastle	W	89r.	90min.	£50

1839
Will Renwick, Shap Fells, Westmorland	W	64r.	75min.	£200

1840
Hammer Lane, Lindrick Common, Notts.	W	52r.	72min.	£200

Again there was a vacuum after Young Molineaux retired and the only probable legitimate claim was that of John Callaghan's after his defeat of John "Solid" Coates in 1845.

143

Nat Langham
(Recognized as the best in the land at a middle weight 1846-1853)

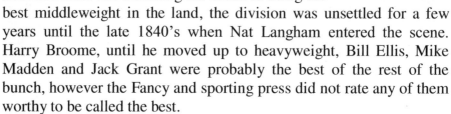

Born: 1820   Died: 1871

"Ould Nat"

Again after Young Molineaux's retirement and Hammer Lane not resuming his claim to being the best middleweight in the land, the division was unsettled for a few years until the late 1840's when Nat Langham entered the scene. Harry Broome, until he moved up to heavyweight, Bill Ellis, Mike Madden and Jack Grant were probably the best of the rest of the bunch, however the Fancy and sporting press did not rate any of them worthy to be called the best.

Nat Langham was 5' 10" tall and weighed around 154lbs. and became another one of the greats of the bare knuckle era, being a tough, agile and scientific boxer. His first recorded fights were wins against William Ellis in eight rounds at Hinkley, Leicestershire in 1843, Tom Lowe at Long Reach, Whitstable, Kent in forty three rounds in 1844 and "Doc" Campbell in twenty seven rounds in 1845. A win over George Gutteridge at Bourne, Lincolnshire in eighty five titanic rounds in 1846 established Langham as the top middleweight around and in the next year, 1847 he was involved in a terrific scrap with the Australian William Sparkes when they met on Woking Common, Surrey taking Nat sixty seven rounds, with Sparks arm broken for the last five rounds, before he was able to subdue the brave Australian, but any doubts as to Nat Langham being acclaimed as the best middleweight in the land were dispelled with this win. It was four years before Langham fought again having suffered lung trouble through suspected consumption, however he returned in 1851 to take on top heavyweight contender Harry Orme at Lower Hope Point, Medway, Kent and in a fight against a much heavier man it was Nat Langham's only defeat during his illustrious career, but it still took Orme one hundred and seventeen rounds to overcome Langham.

By 1853 a fight with the highly rated Tom Sayers was the fight everyone wanted to see and they finally got their wish when the two clashed at Lakenham, Suffolk for the recognition of being called the best middleweight in the land at that time. For sixty rounds these two great warriors stood toe to toe and hammered each other practically senseless, but with Nat Langham very weak from his efforts and Sayers swollen eyes closing fast, one final tremendous effort from Langham was good enough for Sayers seconds to throw in the sponge, it being the only loss of Tom Sayers career, although he was destined for further greatness a few years later.

After this, Nat, who refused to meet Sayers again, announced his retirement and took over the running of the Cambrian Stores pub in Leicester Square, London, but four years later, when he was 37 years old he got caught up in a family row with his brother-in-law, Ben Caunt, the ex-Champion of England, now 43 years old, so they faced each other in the ring and fought out a sixty round draw, shook hands afterwards and buried the hatchet. Dogged with ill health throughout the rest of his life Nat remained landlord of the Cambrian Stores until his death from consumption in 1871 at 51 years of age.

1843
William Ellis, Hinkley, Leics.   W   8r.   20min.   £10

1844
Tom Lowe, Long Reach, Whitstable, Kent   W   43r.   50min.   £25

1845
Doc Campbell, London   W   27r.   35min.   £10

1846
George Guttridge, Bourne, Lincs.   W   85r.   93min.   £50
Now acclaimed as the best middleweight in the country.

1847
William Sparks, Woking Common, Surrey   W   67r.   63min.   £100

1851
Harry Orme, Lower Hope Point, London   L   117r.   166min.   £100

1853
Tom Sayers, Lakenheath, Suffolk   W   61r.   122min.   £200

1857
Ben Caunt, Medway, Kent   D   60r.   89min.   £400

Bob Brettle
(Acclaimed as the best in the land at middleweight 1856-1860)

Born: 1832   Died: 1872

Tom Sayers was considered by most people as the best at middleweight in England since Nat Langham retired after beating Sayers in 1853, however Sayers was more interested in going after the heavier men for the most prized title in pugilism, namely the accolade of being called the Champion of England, although only a middleweight himself. This left Bob Brettle, Jem Mace, Ned "Posh" Price and possibly Job Cobley as the best of the rest at middleweight in the latter half of the 1850's.

Bob Brettle was born in Portobello near Edinburgh in 1833, but lived most of his life in the Black Country of England, working as a glassblower and later, when a prize fighter, he became a publican at the White Lion in Digbeth, Birmingham. A fresh faced, round shouldered, confident character he weighed about 144lbs. and stood just over 5' 7" in his bare feet. He fought out of a crab like stance, ready to spring on to the attack at any time, throwing powerful punches with either fist and became very highly rated around the Midlands.

His first encounter in the prize ring started in 1849 with a loss, but five wins on the trot against minor opponents took him through to 1854 when he met Bob Malpas at Defford Common, Worcestershire and after eighteen rounds of brutal fighting there was a protest from Brettle's corner that their man had been fouled. After lengthy arguments the stakes were drawn and the contest was declared a draw. He then fought Jack Jones at Purfleet, Essex and when darkness halted proceedings after forty nine rounds, Brettle, for some reason refused to continue the next day and so forfeited the purse. In 1855 he beat the highly fancied Roger Coyne at Combe, Warwickshire in forty nine rounds and then the next year at Didcot, Berkshire he beat the durable Sam Simmonds in thirteen rounds to be recognized by many as the best middleweight around apart from Tom Sayers.

Job Cobley known as the "Enthusiastic Pot Boy" was Bob Brettle's next opponent when they met at Shell Haven, Essex in 1857 and after a titanic struggle Brettle emerged as the winner after forty seven rounds, further cementing his claim as the best middleweight around. With this victory under his belt a match was made for him to take on the recognized top lightweight, Bob Travers in 1858 in a catch weight contest with the weight limit being set at ten stone two pounds. The venue was Appledore, Kent and for the first hour of fighting Brettle was the better man, however police broke up the fight after forty rounds had been fought and it was decided to continue the next day. Travers was suffering from heavy bruising and Brettle had a damaged right hand, but after one hundred rounds of fierce fighting Travers was eventually disqualified for a foul.

By 1859 with Sayers now Champion of England and no longer interested in fighting at middleweight, Jem Mace and Bob Brettle were matched against each other, the no nonsense bruiser against the classic skills of Jem Mace, but Mace with a reputation of being either brilliant or somewhat erratic at times. It was the latter Jem Mace that turned up that day at the Medway, Kent, with Brettle knocking Mace out in just two rounds, although both men denied reports of a fixed fight. In 1859 Brettle got his chance to fight the marvellous Tom Sayers which was claimed by Brettle's camp as being for the Championship of Britain, although not recognized by Sayers for any title. The fight turned out to be a very tame affair with Sayers being way too good for Brettle, beating him in seven one sided rounds, which ended with Brettle's shoulder being dislocated from one of Sayer's blows. Brettle was still recognized as the best at middleweight though, as Sayers was only interested in the heavier weight division still and which he was now recognized as champion of since he beat Tom Paddock the year before.

Brettle was now challenged again by Jem Mace and the pair met in pouring rain at Wallingford, Berkshire in 1860, but after police stopped the fight, with Mace the better man after six rounds had been fought, the fight resumed the next day near Southend, Essex. Mace carried on from where he had left off the day before and knocked Brettle out after five rounds to be now recognized as the finest middleweight in the country.

In 1861 Brettle met Jack Rooke at Meopham, Kent but the referee declared the fight a draw after twenty three rounds when police appeared and intervened, which they repeated when the two fighters met at Rainham, Kent the next day, both of these fights being alleged

147

fixed fights. Two months later a further fight between the two, again, allegedly fixed, resulted in another draw when the two of them just circled each other for nearly two hours. With this fight Bob Brettle's illustrious ring career ended rather shabbily and he disappears into obscurity after this.

1849

Ward Freeds, Soltey, Birmingham	L			
Joe Foxall	W			purse

1851

Jack Parkinson	W			

1852

Ed Garvey	W			

1853

Will Canfield	W			
Joe Stone	W			

1854

Ben Malpas, Defford Common, Worcs.	LF/D	88r.		£100
Jack Jones, Purfleet, Essex *(darkness fell)*	L	49r.	105min.	£200

Brettle refused to resume the fight four days later so paid forfeit.

1855

Roger Coyne, Combe, Warks.	WF	49r.	48min.	£50

1856

Sam Simmonds, Didcot, Berks	W	13r.	16min.	£400

Now acclaimed as the best middleweight in the country.

1857

Job Cobley, Shell Haven, Essex	WF	47r.	70min.	£200

1858

Bob Travers, Appledore, Kent *(stopped by police)*	D	42r.	65min.	
Bob Travers, Shell Haven, Kent	W	100r.	120mins.	£200
Jem Mace, Medway, Kent	W	2r.	3min.	£200

1859

Tom Sayers, Leashford, Sussex	L	7r.	15min.	£600

1860

Jem Mace, Wallingford, Berks *(stopped-police)*	D	6r.	12min	
Jem Mace, Essex Marshes, *(continued from previous day)*	L	5r.	7min.	£400+purse

1861

Jack Rooke, Meopham, Kent *(stopped by police)*	D	23r.	75min.	£400
Jack Rooke, Rainham, Kent *(stopped by oolice)*	D	3r.	17min.	£400

1862
Jack Rooke, Aldershot, Hants.   D   4r.   100min. £400

Jem Mace and Tom Sayers are not included here as they are regarded as being in the heavier class and have been described in the previous chapter. Mace, like Sayers relinquished the title of Champion of the Middleweights shortly after beating Bob Brettle to pursue the much more sought after title of Champion of England, although his fight with Joe Goss in 1863 is described in some record books as being for the Middleweight title. However like Sayers he quickly distanced himself from the middleweight scene, although both fighters were at the weight or skill level where they could fight at both weights. The middleweight division began to throw up several fighters now that Mace was no longer interested in defending the title; however it is disputable whether any of them were generally recognized or accepted champions. The men claiming to be the middleweight division champions after Mace were Ned Price in 1861, Joe Goss in 1862, Ned Price again in 1862 until 1865, followed by John Baldock later in 1865, Young Tom Lane in 1866, Bodger Crutchley in 1867 and Tom Kenny later that same year. Bill Matthews was probably the last bare knuckle pugilist in the middleweight class to claim that particular title in 1871.

THE LIGHTWEIGHTS

Men weighing under ten stone or 140lbs. had been fighting since around 1745 but had to take on much heavier men to obtain fights; first class fighters such as Ned Hunt and later in the 1780's Tom Tyne and Bob Watson were notable examples of "men of a lighter weight" which was used to describe them. Towards the 1800's the lightweight classification gradually evolved and was established for men weighing approximately between 126lbs.-140lbs.

The term lightweight was being used by 1821 when Jack Randall ruled at this weight and certainly by 1827 when Dick Curtis was unbeatable by anyone in this class.

Caleb Baldwin
(Acclaimed as the best in the land at a light weight 1801-1804)

Born 1769:   Died: 1827

"The Pride of Westminster"

Around the early 1800's with some good light men around one stood out above the rest. Caleb Baldwin (real name Ramsbottom) was born in Westminster, London and grew up to become a brilliant 5' 6" lightweight, weighing in at about 133lbs. Fighting professionally from the age of 16 his first reported bout was against Jem Gregory on Tooting Fields in 1785, then a week later he defeated Jem Jones. His next fight that year against Gypsy Arthur Smith was a severe test for Baldwin who eventually won when the gypsy was forced to retire. A few weeks later he came up against Jerry Matthews who ran off after 15 minutes! This left Baldwin the winner and shortly after that brief episode he beat a certain Bill Burke in 12 minutes who at least didn't run off! All of these fights were held in or around London.

In 1792 he fought the experienced Paddington Jones to a creditable draw, after which, the fighting fraternity realized that Caleb Baldwin was something special. In late 1792 Bob Packer, an experienced fighter challenged Baldwin and the two met on Hounslow Heath, with Packer forced into defeat after 45 minutes. In December 1800 Baldwin battered Irishman James Kelly to defeat in twelve rounds and in November 1801 at Hurley Bottom near Maidenhead, Berkshire he took on and thrashed butcher Jack Lee in seventeen rounds with most people now accepting Baldwin the best at lightweight in the land. Another Irishman came and went in October 1803, Jack O'Donnell, an experienced pugilist was stopped in round eight on Wimbledon Common. Caleb Baldwin's formidable winning streak came to an end when he met Dutch Sam at Highgate, London in August 1804. There is some dispute as to whether Baldwin was fully fit, however in a dreadfully punishing fight Dutch Sam was the victor in thirty seven rounds. Although Baldwin had the better of the exchanges up to round twenty, dropping Dutch Sam several times, he began to fade and eventually forced to retire, resulting in his only loss in the ring. With this win Dutch Sam was now recognized as the best at lightweight in England. A rematch was made for the next month but Dutch Sam pulled out forfeiting his deposit of 20 guineas.

A year later in August 1805, Baldwin took on Irishman Bill Ryan on Blackheart Common, London in a rough, brawling fight and up to round twenty six neither man gave any quarter, until a foul was called out by Baldwin's supporters. All hell let loose outside the ring, which was destroyed in the battle between the rival supporters, who were eventually quelled when Dragoon Guards arrived. Some record books give this as a draw, others as a win by a foul to Caleb Baldwin and with this fight he retired. Many years later though, in 1816 he came out of retirement to take on Young Massa Bristow at Combe Wood, London and at the grand old age of 47 he showed the young Bristow he had not lost his touch by beating him in thirteen rounds. He then retired for good to become a costermonger, but still acted as a corner man in many later fights. He died in Westminster, London aged 58.

1786

Jem Young, Tothill Fields, London	W		20min.	½gn.
Jem Jones, Wimbledon Common, London	W		15min.	2gns.
Arthur Smith, Kelsey Green, London	W		25min.	10gns.
Jerry Matthews, Hyde Park, London	W		15min.	20gns.
Bill Burke, Bexley Heath, Middlesex	W		12min.	10gns.
Bill Wadhams, Westminster, London	W		60min.	20gns.

1792

Bob Packer, Hounslow Heath, Middlesex	W		45min.	20gns.
Tom Jones, Smitham Bottom, London	D		30min.	£20+purse

1800

James Kelly, Wimbedon, London	W	12r.	15min.	20gns+purse

1801

Jack Lee, Hurley Bottom, Berks.	W	21r.	23min.	100gns.

Now acclaimed as the best lightweight in the country.

1803

Jack O'Donnell, Wimbledon Common, London	W	8r.		100gns.

1804

Dutch Sam, Woodford Green, London	L	37r.	75min.	100gns.

1805

Bill Ryan, Blackheath, London	D	26r.	30min.	

1816

Young Massa Bristow, Combe Wood, London	W	13r.		4gns.

Samuel Elias
(Ring career 1801-1814)

Born: 1775   Died: 1816

"Dutch Sam"

Born Samuel Elias in Petticoat Lane, Whitechapel in London, Dutch Sam is widely considered as the inventor of the uppercut. Standing 5' 6" tall and weighing 133lbs. he only ever lost one fight in the whole of his career and that was a comeback fight six years after he officially retired. As a lightweight who punched like a middleweight he was reputed to be the hardest hitter of all the lightweights at the time and soon run out of men of that weight willing to face him, so he took on middleweights where he wreaked havoc amongst them as well! Dutch Sam was considered pound for pound the greatest bare knuckle fighter of all time by many historians on the subject, although he claimed to train on three glasses of gin, three times a day, seven days a week and allegedly placing bottles of the stuff at strategic points on his training runs!

His first fight was against Bill Baker in October 1801, considered by many as a turn up which he won very quickly. Later that year he was put in with the highly rated and experienced Paddington Jones and although Jones was able to force the early part of the fight Dutch Sam caught him with a tremendous punch that felled Jones and also retirement from the contest.

In 1803 a couple of more fights notably against a man called Shipley at Whitechapel, London and another against a man known only as Warren ended in two more victories. Dutch Sam met the great and unbeaten Caleb Baldwin who was being touted as the best lightweight in the land, in August 1804 at Highgate, London and after nine rounds of hard fighting Baldwin was the better man, although he began to tire, which encouraged Dutch Sam on to the attack and although both men were nearly spent, by round thirty seven it was Caleb Baldwin's seconds who threw in the sponge. It was to be Caleb Baldwin's only defeat and gave Dutch Sam the recognition as the best lightweight in England, although Sam never acknowledged any titles bestowed on him. He then took on Bob Britton, known as "The Star of the West" beating him in 30 rounds at Shepperton Common, Surrey in August 1805. It is claimed in some reports that Sam had been on the gin and was tipsy when he entered the ring and was unprepared. The fight was after the Hen Pearce v. Tom Carte battle and was a subscription contest hastily arranged on the spot, with Britton unrecognized, as he was dressed as a country yokel and kidded Sam into thinking that! When, after several rounds he recognized Britton as a professional pugilist Sam knocked him all over the ring!

In February 1806 Sam took on the middleweight Tom Belcher at Moulsey Hurst, Surrey, defeating him in fifty seven titanic rounds. Dissatisfied with the result, Belcher demanded a return, which came about at the same place in July 1807 and another epic battle ensued in which these two great gladiators gave their all, but in round thirty four after a disputed foul blow the contest was declared a draw. A third and deciding contest was staged a month later at Lowfield Common, near Crawley, Sussex where Dutch Sam pummelled Belcher into submission in thirty six rounds, resulting in Dutch Sam being generally recognized as not only the best lightweight in England, but the best middleweight as well. Still Sam never laid claim to any of these titles or accolades and yet no one came forward at either lightweight or middleweight to challenge him!

Dutch Sam then met Bill Cropley, another middleweight and over a stone heavier than him, in May 1808 and he disposed of Cropley in 25 minutes. In May 1810, although being inactive in the ring for two years and probably now being a full blown middleweight himself, Dutch Sam handed out a terrible beating to the much heavier Ben Medley in forty nine rounds on the large. grassy common of Moulsey Hurst, Surrey.

Sam decided to retire at the age of 35 suffering from the wear and tear of hard fighting and drinking, but in December 1814 and out of condition he was coaxed out of retirement at the age of 41 to suffer the only defeat in his spectacular ring career, losing in 50 minutes to the younger Bill Nosworthy, a baker by trade. Sam never got over the defeat to a man who, in Dutch Sam's prime would not even have been mentioned in the same breath.

He began drinking even more heavily and eighteen months later in 1816, after being taken ill, the legend that was Dutch Sam died in a London hospital at the age of 41.

1801

Bill Baker *(turn-up)*	W			5gns.
Tom Jones, Wimbledon Common, London	W			

1803

Shipley, Whitechapel, London	W		15min.	50gns.
Warren, Woodford Green, London	W			

1804

Caleb Baldwin, Woodford Green, London	W	37r.	75min.	50gns.

Now acclaimed as the best lightweight in the country.

1805

Bob Britton, Shepperton, Middx.	W	30r.		£50

1806

Tom Belcher, Sendon Heath, London	W	57r.		100gns.

1807

Tom Belcher, Moulsey Hurst, Surrey	D	34r.		200gns.
Tom Belcher, Lowfield Common, Sussex	W	36r.	56min.	200gns.

Now acclaimed as the best middleweight in the country although still a lightweight.

1808

Bill Cropley, Markyate Street, Herts.	W		25min.	100gns.

1810

Ben Medley, Moulsey Hurst, Surrey	W	49r.	52min.	200gns.

1814

Bill Nosworthy, Moulsey Hurst, Surrey	L	38r.	50min.	£100+purse

Barney Aaron
(Ring career 1819-1834)

Born: 1800   Died: 1859

"Star of the East"

Barney Aaron was born in Aldgate, London right at the beginning of the 19th century growing up to be 5' 6" in height and weighing around 140lbs. and blessed with ability as a skilful, fast and heavy hitting pugilist. He started off as a lightweight with his first recorded fight in 1819 against Bill Connolly at an unknown place in London, winning in sixteen rounds. In between 1820-1822 it is recorded that he fought the heavier and taller Manny Lyons twice, winning one and losing one, winning against the useful Ely Bendon and Samuel Belasco, brother of Aby Belasco and then drawing with Angel Hyams, nephew of Daniel Mendoza, when magistrates stopped the contest after seven rounds.

Now with a growing reputation around the London area young Barney next took on middleweight Tom Collins in 1823 at Moulsey Hurst, but had to retire after 30 minutes with an apparently injured hand when winning. Because of his good showing though he was entered into the lists to fight Ned Stockman at Blindlow Heath, Sussex, beating Stockman, who he severely punished, in thirty nine rounds and further enhancing his credentials with the Fancy. He was next matched with the experienced Jack Lenney at Harpenden Common, Hertfordshire in which Lenney had the better of the early rounds, but Aaron took over, finishing Lenney off in eleven rounds. Not happy with the outcome of this fight Lenney challenged Aaron to a return contest at Moulsey Hurst, Surrey a few months later where Aaron finally got the better of his antagonist again, this time in twenty one rounds.

Frank Redmond was Barney Aaron's next opponent when they also met at Moulsey Hurst, Redmond was never in the fight and was floored after twenty nine rounds. 1824 started with a challenge from Peter Warren and they faced each other at Colnbrook,

Buckinghamshire where the skill of Aaron shone through against his game opponent, with Warren unable to come up to the scratch after twenty nine rounds. Arthur Matthewson who had never been beaten after twenty three recorded fights, including a win the previous year against Aby Belasco, a fellow Jewish compatriot of Aaron's, faced him, with Colnbrook again being the venue, where after a fight that waged one way then the other, a terrific blow to the throat of Aaron in round fifty eight ended the fight for the Jew.

After a fight with kingpin Dick Curtis failed to materialize because he claimed to have turned up at the wrong venue, Aaron is not reported as fighting again until 1826 when he took on and beat Dick Hares at No Man's Land, Hertfordshire in forty three rounds. Aaron was now touting himself at the best of the lightweights, because Dick Curtis the generally acclaimed top man was inactive that year. Curtis had stated previously that he would fight anyone within seven pounds of his own weight of 126lbs. although Aaron was around 10 stone 140lbs. This was soon overcome, and the contest everyone wanted to see was arranged for the following year, 1827 at Andover, Hampshire. In this epic fight the early rounds were pretty even, both men being cautious and showing their respect for each other's boxing skills, but from round five, after being forced through the ropes, Curtis was in the ascendency and a terrific left to Aaron's throat in round nine ended the fight and his claim as the best lightweight.

Old adversary Frank Redmond was now Barney Aaron's next challenger, the pair clashing at No Man's Land, Hertfordshire, where once again Aaron was the better man winning after forty two rounds. In 1828 he fought Marsh Bateman at Lansdowne Racecourse, Dublin beating Bateman in thirty five rounds, then four months later, back in England he was completely outclassed when he lost to the middleweight Harry Jones in eighteen rounds at The Barge House, Woolwich, London. In 1829 he beat the clever and experienced Jem Raines at Navestock Green, Essex in thirteen rounds and there are no other reported fights for Aaron until 1834. In that year in what was to be his last fight at Greenstreet Green, Kent, against middleweight Tom Smith the "East End Sailor Boy", the man who was dubbed the "Star of the East" lost in twenty rounds.

After he retired Barney Aaron could often be seen as an attendant at ringside while carrying on his trade as a fishmonger until his death at 59 years old.

1819

Bill Connelly, London	W	16r.	33min.

1820-1822

Manny Lyons	L	.	75min.
Manny Lyons	W		50min.
Ely Bendon, Bow Common, London	W		45min.
Samuel Belasco	W		
Angel Hyams (stopped by police)	D	7r.	

1823

Tom Collins, Moulsey Hurst, Surrey	L		30min.	purse
Ned Stockman, Blindlow Heath, Sussex	W	39r.	40min.	£50
Jack Lenney, Harpenden Common, Herts.	W	11r.	15min.	£50
Jack Lenney, Moulsey Hurst, Surrey	W	21r.	20min.	£40
Frank Redmond, Moulsey Hurst, Surrey	W	29r.	32min.	£50

1824

Peter Warren, Colnbrook, Bucks.	W	29r.	23min.	£100
Arthur Matthewson, Colnbrook, Bucks.	L	58r.	70min.	£200

1826

Dick Hares, No Man's Land, Herts.	W	43r.		£100

1827

Dick Curtis, Andover, Hants.	L	7r.	50min.	£200
Frank Redmond, No Man's Land, Herts.	W	42r.	72min.	£100

1828

Marsh Bateman, Lansdowne Racecourse Dublin	W	35r.	45min.	£45
Harry Jones, Old Barge House, Woolwich London	L	18r.	15min.	£100

1829

Jem Raines, Navestock Green, Essex	W	13r.	28min.	£100

1834

Tom Smith, Greenstreet Green, Kent	L	20r.	26min.	£100

Dick Curtis
(Acclaimed as the best in the land at lightweight 1823-1828)

Born: 1802   Died: 1843

"The Pet of the Fancy"

During the first two decades of the nineteenth century, after Dutch Sam moved up to wreak havoc amongst the men of the middle weight and Caleb Baldwin had retired, there was no one who could really put the lightweight division on the map until around 1820 when several top flight lightweights emerged almost at the same time, including Jack Lenney, Jack Tisdale, Ned Brown and Barney Aaron. There was none as good as Dick Curtis though, who became another all-time great of the bare knuckle era and the great favourite of the London Prize Ring, hence his title of "The Pet of the Fancy". The Pet stood only 5' 6" and weighing 126lbs. but packed a phenomenal talent and skill into that slight frame. The dangers of being a bare knuckle fighter left Curtis undaunted even though it caused the death of an older brother, Jack, who had died after a bruising contest with Ned Brown.

In June 1820 and still only seventeen he gave a drubbing to a youth called Watson who hailed from Westminster in London, at Moulsey Hurst, Surrey, who was two stone heavier! He once again fought Ned Brown in August 1820 at Maidstone, Kent, who four years earlier was involved in the fight that caused the death of Dick's older brother, Jack. He defeated Brown after an hour of rough and bloody fighting and then in October 1821 he came up against the highly rated Jack Lenney, who was completely overwhelmed after 30 minutes, again the venue being Moulsey Hurst. After beating a so called cousin of Gypsy Jack Cooper in seven rounds at Epsom Downs in May 1822 he followed this by fighting a man who he was destined to face five times in the ring over the next three years, the Cornishman Peter Warren. In ten rounds at Colnbrook, near Slough, in July of the same year, he demolished the game man from the West Country and Curtis was now generally recognized as the king of the lightweights, especially when he met Peter Warren twice more in 1823, defeating him quite easily the first time and then to a draw the second time when the stakes had to be withdrawn due to a dispute.

It was now considered that there was no one in the land at his weight that could beat him and with this in mind in April 1824 at Shepperton, Surrey, Curtis took on the much heavier Dick Hares, however police intervened and so they met up again the next month at Moulsey Hurst, Surrey where Curtis battered Hares to defeat within three rounds. A quick win in two rounds over Ned Stockman in his next fight and he was lined up again against his old adversary once more, Peter Warren in May and July 1825, Curtis winning in five rounds and seven rounds respectively.

A win over Ned Savage proved that Dick Curtis was now almost untouchable, although London's East End favourite, Barney Aaron thought differently. A highly rated fighter, the much heavier Aaron and Curtis couldn't agree to a weight limit, so their fight was declared to be a catch weight contest and in February 1827, at Andover, Hampshire they faced each other. After an even first five rounds Curtis began to get on top from round six and when he unleashed a powerful left to Barney Aaron's throat in round nine, Aaron dropped like a stone and failed to recover in time. His next contest against Jack Tisdale in October the same year at Staines, Surrey resulted in Dick Curtis winning in seventeen rounds and with no willing challengers left Curtis decided to retire.

A year later after trading insults with a fighter called Jack Perkins he was challenged by Perkins to settle their differences in the ring. Confident of beating Perkins, Curtis took the fight at short notice at Hurley Bottom, near Maidenhead, Berkshire in December 1828 and without any significant training, confident that Perkins could not get to him. However, whatever Jack Perkins lacked in the finer points of boxing, durability wasn't one of them and as the fight wore on and Curtis's stamina faded, Perkins took control and in round eleven the inevitable happened. A vicious roundhouse right caught Curtis on the side of the head and he dropped to the ground almost senseless and the most brilliant lightweight of the era was beaten. Curtis retired again, this time for good, adding weight to the saying that they never come back.

1820

Jack Watson, Moulsey Hurst, Surrey	W		25min.	5gns.
Ned Brown, Wimbledon Common, London	W	15r.	57min.	£40

1821

Jack Lenney, Moulsey Hurst, London	W	29r.	38min.	50gns.

1822

George Cooper, Epsom Downs, Surrey	W	7r.	15min.	18gns+purse
Peter Warren, Colnbrook, Berks	W	10r.	20min.	£60

1823

Peter Warren, Moulsey Hurst, Surrey	D	12r.	16min.	£50
Peter Warren, Crawley Downs, Sussex	W	1r.	9min.	£100

Now acclaimed as the best lightweight in the country.

1824

Dick Hares, Moulsey Hurst, Surrey	W	3r.	20min.	£100

1825

Peter Warren, Epsom Downs, Surrey	W	6r.	8min.	£40
Peter Warren, Stanfield Park, Warwicks.	W	7r.	16min.	£190
Ned Savage, Castle Tavern, London (turn-up)	W	16r.	16min.	

1826

Ned Stockman, Highgate Archway, London (turn-up)	W	1r.	7min.	

1827

Barney Aaron, Andover, Hants	W	9r.	50min.	£200
Jack Tisdale, Staines, Middlesex	W	17r.	58min.	£220

1828

George Philips, Blackfriars Inn, London (turn-up)	W	5r.	20min.	
Jack Perkins, Hurley Bottom, Berks.	L	11r.	23min	£200

Owen Swift
(Acclaimed as the best in the land at lightweight 1834-1838)

Born: 1814   Died: 1879

"Little Wonder"

A Londoner, Owen Swift is considered as the next truly acclaimed best lightweight of England after Dick Curtis retired. 1810. Swift stood just 5' 4" and weighed between 126lbs.-128lbs. and was lauded as one of the most skilful little fighters in prize ring history. He made his début in the prize ring at the tender age of fifteen when he defeated Tom McKeever at Primrose Hill, London in 1829 after three rounds and followed this up with another win against Jem Cooper at Egham Racecourse, Surrey in nine rounds. His first loss of only two recorded defeats in the prize ring came at The Barge House, London in 1830, against older and much heavier Tom Smith, but it still took Smith twenty nine rounds to subdue Swift. However, he bounced back with a win over Bill Isaacs in fourteen rounds.

His next fight was against the also highly rated Anthony Noon, a youth of exceptional durability and strength. When they met at Colney Heath, Hertfordshire in 1832 it was a pretty even fight but eventually Swift got the decision after a controversial foul after sixty five rounds and over two hours of fighting. Further wins in the same year against Jem Collins at Whetstone, Kent in twenty one rounds and Ned Brown at Colney Heath, Hertfordshire in twelve rounds propelled young Owen Swift into the limelight and lauded as the local champion around the London area at just twenty years old.

After a win in 1833 against Jack Allen at Whetstone, Kent in forty one rounds, tragedy struck in Owen Swift's next contest against William Murray, when, two weeks after beating Murray in fifty two rounds, Murray was found dead. He was drunk and had apparently fell in a ditch on Waltham Green, London and drowned. In March 1834 at Newport Pagnell, Buckinghamshire, Swift went in with Bill Atkinson who was recognized as the Midlands champion and apart from being game, Atkinson was tough and it took the superior Owen Swift thirty two rounds to finally dispose of him and along with this victory it recognized Swift as the best of the lightweights in the country.

Anthony Noon who Swift had defeated previously, had put an unbeaten string of victories together and disputed the fact that Swift was the rightful champion, so the two recognized top lightweight icons in England met in July 1834 at Andover, Wiltshire It was a titanic struggle and after seventy rounds both men could hardly stand, however Swift's punching finally overcame the game Noon who could take no more after round seventy three. Taken to Andover Anthony Noon never recovered from his injuries and died the next day. Swift was found guilty for causing his death, sentenced and spent the next six months in prison.

Swift did not fight again until he met the highly rated and much heavier "Hammer" Lane in May in which Lane outgunned his much lighter opponent, but it still took one hundred and four rounds for him to beat Swift. Again Swift took some time out before meeting up with the also highly rated Izzy Lazarus in June 1837 at Royston, Hertfordshire and in another great fight Lazarus was eventually overcome after one hundred and thirteen rounds. Again at Royston in March 1838 Owen Swift faced "Brighton" Bill Phelps and it was an evenly fought fight until the superior punching of Swift wore Phelps down to the point that he was finally finished when he collapsed in round eighty five. Unfortunately Phelps died from his injuries three days later and Swift fled to France along with his pal Young Dutch Sam to avoid the law, who, in his absence found Swift guilty of death by manslaughter.

Swift later made his way back to England dressed as a woman, but gave himself up to the English courts immediately on arrival and was acquitted. It was this fight with Phelps that helped bring about the London Prize Ring Rules in 1838 aiming to make the sport fairer and safer and replacing Broughton's Rules that had been in place for nearly 100 years.

Owen Swift did not fight again, got married and took over The Horseshoe, Titchbourne Street in London. In later years he sponsored, backed and refereed fights, ending up as a well-respected man until his death in 1879.

1829

Tom McKeever, Primrose Hill, London	W		60 min.	£3
Jem Cooper, Egham Racecourse, Surrey	W	9r.	25 min.	£14+purse

1830

Tom Smith, Barge House, Woolwich, London	L	29r.	30min.	£20
Bill Isaacs, Harpenden Common, Herts.	W	14r.	22min.	£35+purse

1832

Anthony Noon, Colney Heath, Herts.	WF	65r,	130min.	£50
Jem Collins, Whetstone, Kent	W	21r.	27min.	£20
Ned Brown, Colney Heath, Herts.	W	12r.	24min.	£20

1833

Jack Allen, Whetstone, Kent	W	41r.	100min.	£30
William Murray, Combe Warren, London	W	52r.	77min.	£50
Phil Eyles, Wimbledon Common, London	W	16r.	33min.	£40

1834

Bill Atkinson, Slough, Berks.	W	32r.	40min.	£100

Now acclaimed as the best lightweight in the country.

Anthony Noon, Andover, Hants.	W	73r.	126min.	£100

1836

Hammer Lane, Four Shire Stone	L	104r.	123min.	£100

1837

Izzy Lazurus, Royston, Herts.	W	113r.	135min.	£200

1838

Bill Phelps, Royston, Herts.	W	85r.	95min.	£100
Jack Adams, Bois de Boulogne, France	W	2r.		£100
Jack Adams, Villiers, France	W	34r.	75min.	£100

Jack Hannan
(Ring career 1837-1841)

Born: 1817   Died: 1857

Born in the area of St. Giles, London, nothing is known of Johnny Hannan's boyhood or early life, although we know he grew up to a fighting weight of around 130lbs. and 5' 5" tall and as a lightweight only went in with some of the very best of the lighter men of that period. Hannan was a fast, mobile and expert ring general relying heavily on his speed as his punching was not that powerful, probably accounting for the long duration of his contests.

Jack Hannan's first recorded fight was against the useful Dan Dismore at Cockfoster's, London in 1837, a contest he won over twenty three long rounds lasting just over an hour. In 1838 he came up against the more experienced Tom Maley at the Halfway House, Gravesend where he lost, when, in round eleven he struck Maley when he was on his knees and was disqualified, although at the time he was the favourite to win the contest.

Great things were being expected of the skills of Johnny Walker, making his début in the prize ring when he faced Jack Hannan at Wheeler's End, Oxfordshire in late 1838 putting up a terrific and brave fight before going down to Hannan's speedy fists in thirty one rounds, lasting just under three hours duration. So much was thought of Walker's bravery and skill in his début that he was given a return five months later at Newmarket, Norfolk, when once again after thirty nine rounds lasting just under four hours this time Walker was once again narrowly defeated.

Hannan's next fight ended in defeat to the much heavier Byng Stocks, a middleweight, in eight rounds when they clashed at Royston Heath, Hertfordshire. In 1840 at Melton Mowbray, Leicestershire he beat the tough and useful Jack Forsey in sixteen rounds and with this win propelled himself into the limelight for a meeting with the formidable and unbeaten Johnny Broome, in what was considered by most as a contest between the two best lightweights in the country. The venue chosen was New Park Farm, on the Buckinghamshire border with Oxfordshire, where the two men faced each other in 1841, with Broome the taller man and with a longer reach. After a long pretty even first round Johnny Broome started to prove from then on that he was the stronger man with the more powerful punching power and gradually wearing Jack Hannan down, although he battled on for 79 minutes until having to submit, as he was nearly senseless, although still standing and unable to defend himself anymore. Johnny Broome was now recognized as the best lightweight in the land. Jack Hannan never entered the ring again.

1837

Dan Dismore, Cockfoster's, London	W	23r.	62min.	£50

1838

Tom Maley, Halfway House, Gravesend, Kent	LF	11r.		£50
Johnny Walker, Wheeler's End, Oxon.	W	31r.	174min.	£50

1839

Johnny Walker, Newmarket, Norfolk	W	39r.	228min.	£100
Byng Stocks, Royston Heath, Herts.	L	8r.	93min.	£50

1840

Jack Forsey, Melton Mowbray, Leics.	W	16r.	75min.	£50

1841

Johnny Broome, New Park Farm, Oxon./Bucks	L	47r.	79min.	£1,000

Johnny Broome
(Acclaimed as the best in the land at lightweight 1841-1842)

Born: 1818   Died: 1855

"Young Duckro"

With no recognised claimant as the best lightweight in the land after Owen Swift retired, the leading men vying for top position by 1840 were Sam Merryman, Tom Maley, Johnny Hannan, the promising Johnny Walker and Johnny Broome. Now 24, standing about 5' 7" and weighing 138lbs. Broome was undefeated in seven fights starting with Tom Ellis at an unknown venue near Birmingham around 1832. He then went on to defeat Bill Howell, drew with Jack Hunt and then beat Charles Spilbury, Bob Gallett and the experienced Charlie Jones, all around the Birmingham area from 1833-1839 and although hardly known in London, Broome was highly rated around his own area in the Midlands.

In 1840 Broome travelled up to Glasgow to face the highly respected James McGinty, defeating him in a terrific and long seventy one round fight At just under 140lb. Broome was a bit on the heavy side for a lightweight, but he fought the top class heavyweight Joe Bostock, a man two stone heavier than himself and knocked Bostock out in twelve rounds at Early in Warwickshire later that year. Jack Hannan, a master ring general, was considered the top dog in the London area having twice defeated the up and coming and highly rated Johnny Walker, although Walker was just starting out on his road to fame. After a certain amount of quibbling over a weight limit that was agreeable to both of them, as Hannan was a lighter man, Broome and Hannan eventually met in January 1841 at New Park Farm, Oxfordshire for a reputed £1,000 purse in what was considered to decide the top lightweight in the country. It turned out that Broome's longer reach was too much for Hannan from the outset and Jack Hannan took heavy punishment, until after forty seven rounds he had fought himself to a standstill and being in a terrible physical state, could not continue. Jack Hannan never fought again and because he was getting married, Johnny Broome also retired, with Johnny Walker assuming Broome's accolade of best lightweight by defeating Fred Mason over sixty three rounds in January 1842.

Broome's retirement did not last long however as he was challenged by John Gorrick, an Australian who had arrived in England and although not an aborigine by birth, fought under the name of "Bungaree" an aborigine name. But Bungaree was no match for Johnny Broome when they met up in April 1842 at Mildenhall, Suffolk and he was defeated in forty two rounds of a fight that only lasted 52 minutes. With this win Broome retired for good this time round and became landlord of the Rising Sun, Piccadilly in London. He was also a respected match-maker whose outstanding protégé was his younger brother, Harry, a future Champion of England.

Johnny Broome died at the age of 37 unbeaten in the prize ring

Undated
Tom Ellis, Birmingham	W	6r.	30min.	£10

1833
Bill Howell, Allerbury Common, Worcs.	W	9r.	75min.	£10

1834
Jack Hunt	D		220min.	

1835
Charles Spilsbury, Sutton Coldfield, W. Midlands	W	30r.	63min.	£20

1838
Bob Gallett, Witton, Worcs.	W	9r.	35min.	£20

1839
Charley Jones, Woore, Cheshire	W	31r.	36min.	£100

1840
James McGinty, Glasgow	W	71r.	153min.	£60
Joe Bostock, Early, Warwicks.	W	29r.	47min.	£100

1841
Jack Hannan, New Park Farm, Oxon.	W	47r.	79min.	£1000

Now acclaimed as the best lightweight in the country.

1842
John Gorrick, Newmarket, Suffolk	W	42r.	57min.	£600

Johnny Walker
(Acclaimed as the best in the land at lightweight 1842-1848)

Born: 1819   Died: 1888

Johnny Walker (real name Johnny Badman), born in London, was a well-built, fast, two fisted hard hitter, standing 5' 5" and weighing 133lbs. but was overmatched in his first fight when at just 19 years old he took on the experienced Jack Hannan at Wheelers End, Oxfordshire in November 1838, losing in thirty one rounds. A return in April 1839 near Newmarket, Suffolk saw him lose again, this time in thirty nine rounds after dislocating his shoulder. Two years lapsed before, in June 1841 he beat the highly respected Bill Jones in thirty five rounds at Bray, Berkshire and then in January 1842 at Bagshot, Surrey he outgunned the tough and durable Fred Mason in a brutal contest lasting sixty two rounds, confirming him to many as the top lightweight in the country, with Johnny Broome having retired. With this accolade Walker's next fight was against the up and coming Ned Adams, but not being able to agree to an accepted weight limit the contest was made at catch weight and held at Bracknell, Berkshire in July 1842. Walker and Adams were evenly matched; first Walker then Adams having the upper hand, but heavy rain drained both fighters strength until Adams could no longer continue after round forty four.

Walker retired claiming to be the champion of the lightweights and several attempts were made to persuade him back, but all failed until he was coaxed back into the prize ring to fight the promising and unbeaten Sam Simmonds. They duly met at Lakenheath, Suffolk in December 1846 with Walker winning easily in thirteen rounds ending the fight with a powerful right. With this Walker again announced himself as the undisputed top lightweight in the country but this announcement was next challenged by a new rising star, the heavier Tom Lane, a younger brother to the famous "Hammer" Lane. The fight was to be at catch weight, but Walker had to pay a forfeit as the contest had to be called off due to Walker being ill with the flu. The contest was rearranged for February 1848 at Hythe, Kent and from the start Walker was not fighting in his usual style; in fact he apparently seemed lethargic and clumsy. Twice he was nearly disqualified and in round thirteen after a warning from his seconds to start fighting properly, to the amazement of everyone present including his opponent, he walked out of the ring! Walker later complained that he had hurt his thumb; many people thought it was a fix and all bets were declared void, robbing Tom Lane of an apparently deserved victory, although compensated for his troubles as he was the innocent party.

Walker relinquished his claim as the best of the lightweights when later that year he travelled to the USA with his brother Alf and on his return in 1853 a contest with Bill Hayes fell through when Walker declined to fight and again in 1854 when he was absent at the appointed fight time. However, it was finally fixed for December 1854 but the contest was more like an exhibition as the two evenly matched fighters styles cancelled each other out, eventually darkness was the winner and although a continuation was arranged for a later date it never materialized. Walker now 39 was due to fight Bob Travers in 1858 but again forfeited a fight complaining of lumbago this time. Johnny Walker was to never fight again.

Unknown
"Navvy" Grant, Globe Lane, London   W   60min.

1838
Johnny Hannan, Wheeler's End, Oxon.   L   31r.   174min. £50

1839
Johnny Hannan, Newmarket, Suffolk   L   39r.   228min. £100

1841
Bill Jones, Bray, Berks.   W   35r.   57min.   £100

1842
Fred Mason, Bagshot, Surrey   W   42r.   75min.   £120
Now acclaimed as the best lightweight in the country.
Ned Adams, Bracknell, Berks.   W   44r.   83min.   £200

1846
Sam Simmonds, Lakenheath, Suffolk   W   13r.   31min.   £400

1848
Tom Lane, Hythe, Folkstone, Kent   D   12r.   15min.   £400

1855
Bill Hayes, Appledore, Kent   D   36r.   148min   £400

Ned Donnelly
(Acclaimed as the best in the land at lightweight 1852-1853)

Born: 1828   Died: 1860

By 1850, with the disgraced Johnny Walker in America the four top lightweights in Britain were probably Ned Donnelly, Jack Jones, Bill Hayes and Mike Madden. Ned Donnelly stood 5' 6½" and weighed about 132 lbs. and was a native of Glasgow in Scotland and who had started his ring career in 1845 with a win against an unknown collier in a mammoth one hundred and eight rounds at Dalmarnock Bridge, Glasgow and from then until 1848 he beat Archie McNeil, Angus McKay, Jim Clarke and Ned James, the last two men at Atley, Lancashire and Point of Ayr, Wales respectively.

In 1849 he ventured south to London where on Dartford Marshes, London he carried on his winning ways stopping Dan Collins in round seventy eight. In March 1851 Jack Jones was beaten by Mike Madden in a fight which brought two hard hitting opponents together in a toe to toe battle, with Madden, in the end, possessing the heavier punches. In the same year Ned Donnelly drew with Bill Hayes at Lower Hope, Tilbury, London and when in atrocious weather, darkness beat them, they agreed to continue at a later date to be arranged, as Donnelly had hurt his foot when Bill Hayes spiked shoe had accidentally stabbed it. When they did resume two months later they fought in blazing hot sun, but their opposite styles cancelled each other out and after nineteen rounds in over three hours, both fighters shook hands on a draw.

Donnelly lost his first recorded fight to George Brown on a foul in April 1852 at Long Reach, London and seven years after his debut in the prize ring. In 1851 Bill Hayes had beaten Jack Jones and in December 1852 the long awaited Donnelly-Madden fight resulted in a win for Donnelly, after Madden was disqualified in round sixty eight. This win resulted in Ned Donnelly being recognized by many as the top lightweight in the land although, of course, Bill Hayes, Jack Jones and probably Mike Madden didn't agree. Jones immediately threw down a challenge to Donnelly and while Jones trained hard for the fight at Tilbury, London in March 1853, Donnelly didn't and it was only his boxing skills that kept him in the fight with darkness eventually saving him to earn a draw. In a return match three months later in June at Brandon Heath, Norfolk, Donnelly made sure he was in top shape to overcome Jones, resulting in Ned Donnelly showing his mastery of the finer points of boxing against the cruder tactics of Jack Jones. After being on top for thirty four rounds Donnelly was suddenly caught by an explosive punch by Jones and knocked cold and Jack Jones after many years and ring wars had finally won top spot as king of the lightweights.

1845

An unknown Collier, Glasgow	W	108r.	128min.	£4
Archie McNeil, Glasgow	W	80r.	190min.	

1846

Angus McKay, Glasgow	W	9r.	26min.	£50

1848

Jim Clarke, Astley, Lancs.	W	37r.	160min.	£20
Ned James, Point of Ayr, North Wales	W	9r.	17min.	£40

1849

Dan Collins, Dartford Marshes, Kent	W	78r.	184min.	£50

1851

Bill Hayes, Lower Hope Point, Kent	D	39r.	145min.	£200
Bill Hayes, Six Mile Bottom, Suffolk	D	19r.	195min.	£200

1852

George Brown, Long Reach, Kent	LF	15r.	42min.	£45
Mike Madden, Long Reach, Kent	W	68r.	130min.	£100

Now acclaimed as the best lightweight in the country.

1853

Jack Jones, East Tilbury, London	D	48r.	136min.	£100
Jack Jones, Brandon Heath, Suffolk	L	35r.	126min.	£200

Jack Jones
(Acclaimed as the best in the land at lightweight 1853)

Born: 1821   Died: 1854

Jack Jones was born in Portsmouth and his real surname was Humphries and why he changed it to Jones is a mystery, although people did to avoid the law for one reason or another. He was apparently a man who knew no fear in the ring and fought for the sheer love of it as well as for the purses, standing 5' 8" and weighing 136lbs. he was a handful for any opponent. He won several fights along the south coast of England until he came up against and was beaten by the heavier Joe Rowe at Salisbury.

He came to London in 1850 where he beat the highly rated George Crockett before going down to the top rated Mike Madden in a brutal, slugging contest in March 1851. Later in 1851 Jones agreed to meet Bill Hayes another top class fighter at Horley, Surrey and though in a fight where Hayes was always the better man, it was darkness that beat them in the end, although Jones was so tired by round one hundred and one that he mistook one of Hayes seconds for his opponent! It was at this point the referee intervened and called it a day. In March 1853 Jones agreed to meet Ned Donnelly, the generally recognized best lightweight in the country at Tilbury, Essex and thinking he easily had the beating of Jones, Donnelly did not train properly for the fight. Donnelly started well against the more aggressive Jones however he was also the first to tire which encouraged Jones to redouble his efforts, however after more than two hours it was again darkness that beat both fighters and a draw was agreed. Although there was no resumption of the fight the next day it was agreed that a return should be arranged for a later date and so in June of that same year of 1853 they faced each other again at Brandon Heath, Suffolk. A fully fit Ned Donnelly was by far the better man this time as he slashed Jones to ribbons, but Jones would not give in and by round thirty five Donnelly was also very tired, when suddenly from nowhere, Jones landed a terrific right that pole-axed Donnelly and Jack Jones was now considered to have earned the title of being the top lightweight.

Bill Hayes, who had drawn with Jones two years earlier, then challenged Jones and in November 1853 they met at Mildenhall, Suffolk and after three hours, with the aggressive style of Jones cancelling out the hit and run tactics of Hayes, a halt was called until the next day because of impending darkness. There was no sign of Jones the next day and so Hayes was declared the winner and so assumed the mantle of champion of the lightweights. In 1854 Jones beat Bob Brettle under the same circumstances and then, when fighting Mike Madden, he struck his head on a ring stake, was carried out of the ring to the nearest tavern where he died later that day.

Undated
Jones was the winner of fights against Brown, Hayes, Bosworth, Tom Jenkins and other unknown opponents. No other details are known.

1846

Ted Hill, Havant, Sussex	W	18r.		

1847

Will Cole, Hayling Island, Hants.	W	20r.	19min.	£40

1849

Joe Rowe, Salisbury, Wilts.	L	18r.	46min.	£50

1850

Harry Martin, Lower Hope Point, Kent	W	29r.	58min.	£60
George Crockett, Grays, Essex	W	7r.	38min.	£100

1851

Mike Madden, Long Reach, Kent	L	29r.	65min.	£100
Bill Hayes, Horley, Surrey	L	101r.	237min.	£100

1853

Ned Donnelly, East Tilbury, London	D	48r.	136min.	£100
Ned Donnelly, Brandon Heath, Suffolk	W	35r.	126min.	£200
Now acclaimed as the best lightweight in the country.				
Bill Hayes, Mildenhall, Suffolk	D	72r.		
Bill Hayes, Tilbury, London	L		183min.	£400

1854

Bob Brettle, Purfleet, Essex	W	49r.	105min.	£200

1855

Mike Madden, Long Reach, Kent	L	23r.	69min.	£100

Bill Hayes
Acclaimed as the best in the land at lightweight 1853-1857)

Born: 1827   Died: 1859

A tall man, at 5' 8" and weighing 136lbs. slightly built and fair haired, Bill Hayes was born in London and built up a reputation as a scientific boxer who had won five contests in the London area, the last three against top class opposition.

Because of his defensive style of fighting, many of Hayes fights were long in duration. When he came up against Mike Madden at Edenbridge, Kent in July 1849 the contest resulted in being the longest in prize fighting history with Madden losing after one hundred and eighty five rounds in just over six hours of fighting. He next fought Alec Keene early in 1851 in the Forest of Dean and because of a medical condition which had left him blind in one eye after the Madden fight, Hayes over his cautiousness and defensive tactics resulted in him being ruled out after forty five rounds for continuously dropping on one knee. In March 1851 in atrocious conditions of sleet, rain and mud at Lower Hope Point, Kent and with darkness closing in, with the two men evenly matched, after forty five rounds it was declared the contest be resumed at a later date. It was to be two months later before the two men faced each other again, this time in blazing hot sun with the fight going much the same way as the first, with both men's styles again cancelling each other out for either to get an outright decision and the contest was declared a draw after another forty five rounds.

Late 1851 saw Bill Hayes fight Jack Jones to a another no decision fight, after nearly four hours of fighting and Hayes didn't fight again until he went up against Jack Grant in February 1853 in another contest that had to be adjourned after seventy three rounds and continued the next month, which after one hundred and fifteen rounds was called to a halt and a draw agreed. In November 1853 Bill Hayes took on Jack Jones, currently generally recognized as the top lightweight in the country, at Mildenhall, Suffolk, with the aggressive Jones attacking and the defensive Hayes being his usual evasive self, resulting in darkness calling a halt to the proceedings until the next day. Jones' camp was not keen on so quick a resumption of proceedings, wanting to give their man more recovery time, but this was overruled. The next day Jones did not show, forfeiting the fight to Hayes and therefore the accolade of the best lightweight in the country was now bestowed by the majority on Hayes.

Johnny Walker, the old recognized champion, returned from America at around the time Hayes was recognized as the new champion, and during Walker's absence talk was of a Hayes-Walker fight if Walker ever returned to these shores, as Walker had not lost his title in the ring. The match was made for May 1854, but as Walker did not show for the weigh-in the fight was awarded to Hayes. Another match was made for December that year at Appledore, Kent and in a biting wind the two fought until darkness with an agreement to resume the affair at a later date but it was never to be and later both fighters announced their retirements from the ring.

Walker definitely retired for good, but Hayes changed his mind. Victory by Jem Massey over Young Norley in April 1856, with Massey claiming to be the new champion bought Bill Hayes out of retirement and up against Massey at Bentley, Suffolk. After 36 rounds the police intervened so it was continued at Ardleigh, Essex, eight miles away and like so many of Hayes fights, again the contest ended in a draw.

Hayes next fight was against the promising young Bob Travers who was becoming a top notch fighter and they met in May 1857 at Medway, Kent. Travers played the long distance game the same as Hayes and so after three hours of almost non-fighting it was the older Bill Hayes who was beginning to tire. Sensing this Travers turned up the heat and in round seventy caught Hayes with a terrific right to the body. Hayes lasted to round seventy seven until caught by another body punch and it was all over, with Bob Travers being recognized as the one that all the others now had to beat to be recognized as the best of the lightweights.

Bill Hayes died two years later.

1847

| Bill Finn, Dartford Marshes, Kent | W | 38r. | 93min. | £10 |
| Harry Cooper, Woking Common, Surrey | W | 45r. | 65min. | £100 |

1848

| Sam Martin, Woking Common, Surrey | W | 28r. | 85min. | £100 |

1849

George Crockett, Lower Hope Point, Kent	W	8r.	98min.	£100
Mike Madden, Edenbridge, Kent	W	185r.	363min.	£200

1850

Alex Keene, Forest of Dean, Gloucs.	LF	45r.	85min.	£200

1851

Ned Donnelly, Lower Hope Point, Kent	D	19r.	145min.	£200
Ned Donnelly, Six Mile Bottom, Suffolk	D	19r.	195min.	£200
Jack Jones, Horley, Surrey	W	101r.	237min.	£100

1853

Jack Grant, Lower Hope Point, Kent	D	73r.	110min.	£200
Jack Grant, East Tilbury, London	D	115r.	204min.	£300
Jack Jones, Mildenhall, Suffolk	D	72r.	183min.	£400
Jack Jones, Tilbury, London	W (Jones absent at start)			

Now acclaimed as the best lightweight in the country.

1855

Johnny Walker, Appledore, Kent	D	36r.	148min.	£400

1856

Jem Massey, Suffolk/Essex border	D	51r.	112min.	£200

1857

Bob Travers, Medway, Kent	L	78r.	225min.	£200

Bob Travers
Acclaimed as the best in the land at lightweight 1857-1863)

Born: 1836   Died: Unknown

"The Black Wonder"

Born in America, Bob Travers moved with his parents to Manchester in England when he was two years old. Weighing 136lbs. and standing 5' 8" tall Travers first contest was under his real surname of Crowhurst, a win against Jem Malvern, after that he fought under the name of Travers.

His first recorded fight was against Jim Malvern in 1854 in Liverpool which he won in forty rounds. Coming to London in 1855 his next fight against George Baker, however four days later they met again Long Reach, Whitstable, Kent where over another ten rounds Travers was the winner. Wins were then recorded over Jesse Hatton at Coombe Bottom, Guildford, Surrey and George Crockett at Egham, Surrey. A defeat against Job Cobley and a win over Bill Cleghorne bought him up against old warrior and acclaimed top lightweight in the land, Bill Hayes, but the old warrior at 30 years old was worn down in seventy rounds by Bob Travers at Medway, Kent in May 1857 and Travers was now generally recognized as king of the lightweights.

With no rivals considered to be a match for him at his weight of about 133lbs. Travers challenged rivals of over 140lbs. and in June 1858 at Appledore, Kent fought Bob Brettle at catch weight, as Brettle was over 140lb. When police stopped the fight it moved to London the next day, where Travers lost on a foul. After victory against Mike Madden in April 1859 after forty five rounds at Ashford, Kent, Travers followed this up in February 1860 with a catch weight contest against top rated Jem Mace and after police intervened, again Travers was disqualified, this time after fifty seven rounds when fighting resumed the next day. Further victories at catch weight against "Bodger" Crutchley and Bos Tyler in 1861 only confirmed Travers as king of the lightweights at 133lb.-140lb.

Over the years that Travers reigned, Bill Gilham at about 120lbs. argued the point, claiming to be the lightweight supremo. As the lightweight limits were generally recognized as between 112lbs. to 140lbs. Travers knowing he could never get down 120lbs. to challenge Gilham, ignored these claims. Giving weight yet again Bob Travers next fought Patsy Reardon at catch weight in July 1862 in Hampshire and after six rounds police once again intervened and so the parties travelled back to London where hostilities continued the next day. Travers was the more scientific fighter and was the better man until the weather changed for the worse, when Reardon gradually got on top and after fifty three rounds and over four hours of fighting the now defenceless Traver's seconds threw in the sponge.

After Jem Dillon's fine showing against Patsy Reardon and as he fought within the generally agreed lightweight limit, a challenge was thrown out to Travers with the claim as to who was the best lightweight in the land out of the two of them being at stake. They met at Twyford, Berkshire in August 1863 and for the first hour the pair were evenly matched when suddenly a warning went out that the police were on their way to spoil things. Hastily moving to a second site the fight continued but Travers hands were now in a bad state and when after sixteen rounds a second warning came that the police were arriving, Travers backers called for a postponement until a later date. The referee refused the request and as Travers was not forthcoming the fight was awarded to Jem Dillon.

Neither man fought again, although for three years after there was talk of a return, in fact articles were drawn up in 1866 but Travers was now well over 30 and as it was well known that Dillon had an aversion to training so the challenge was never taken up by Travers or Dillon.

1854

Jim Malvern, Throstles Nest, Liverpool	W	40r.	90min.	£10

1855

George Baker, Tilbury, London (stopped by police)	D	10r.	23min.	£50
George Baker, Long Reach, Kent	W	10r.	20min.	£50

1856

Jesse Hatton, Coombe Bottom, Surrey	W	39r.	76min.	£50
George Crockett, Egham, Surrey	W	37r.	114min.	£100
Job Cobley, Halfway House, London	L	110r.	200min.	£100

1857

Jack Cleghorn, Long Reach, Kent	W	36r.	87min.	£200
Bill Hayes, Medway, Kent	W	78r.	225min.	£200

Now acclaimed as the best lightweight in the country.

1858

Bob Brettle, Appledore, Kent (stopped by police)	D	42r.	65 min.	£200
Bob Brettle, Shell Haven, Essex	LF	100r.	125 min.	£200

1859

Mike Madden, Ashford, Kent	W	45r.	97min.	£200

1860

Jem Mace, Medway, Kent (stopped by police)	D	6r.	21min.	
Jem Mace, Medway, Kent	LF	57r.	91min.	£200

1861

Bodger Crutchley, Medway, Kent) (stopped by police)	D	3r.	44min.	£100
Bos Tyler, London	W	17r.	63min.	£200

1862

Patsy Reardon, London (stopped by police)	D	7r.	37min.	
Patsy Reardon, London	L	53r	245min.	£200

1863

Jem Dillon, Twyford, Berks	L	54r.	122min.	£400

Bob Travers and Jem Dillon both retired and although there was talk of a return in 1866 it did not materialize. In November 1864 Bos Tyler beat George Crockett and claimed the accolade but this was his last fight as he then retired, James Lead then beat Jerry Hawkes in May 1865 to claim the title, even though police intervened after 11 rounds, but he never fought again after this contest. In April 1866 Tim Collins beat Joe Bent, but as Collins, a second rate fighter had only fought other second raters up until then, including Bent, no one took this claim seriously. Bob Travers was probably the last legitimate claimant of the lightweight title in 1863 to be recognized by the Fancy. Arthur Chambers whose first fight was in 1864 with only one defeat up until 1870 then took on George Fletcher near Prestatyn in North Wales in October of that same year, defeating Fletcher in 56 rounds. After this fight he bestowed the title of Lightweight Champion on himself but only a year later he had emigrated to America where he won the American Lightweight Championship.

FEATHERWEIGHTS

Many fighters weighing under or around the 9 stone mark were finding the weight difference of entering the prize ring with lightweights weighing 126lbs. plus difficult to contend with, so towards the 1850's a weight class gradually came into being representing men weighing under 126lbs. which became known as featherweight. This recognized men who weighed from approximately 116lbs.-126lbs.

Jemmy Massey
(Acclaimed as the best in the land at featherweight 1847)

Born: 1824   Died: 1863

"The Stunted Lifeguardsman"

Jemmy Massey was born in Salford, Manchester and grew to no more than 5' 3" in height, although his fighting weight increased over the years from a starting weight of 112lbs. and receiving his nickname because of his muscular and broad frame. He was a clever, fast and superb body puncher, but he suffered being saddled with a quick temper. In the late 1840's the term "featherweight" began to be used to accommodate those fighters who weighed up to 126lbs. and when Massey beat Young Norley in 1847 he was generally recognized as one the best in this class.

Massey's career in the ring started in 1842 when he faced Jack Cronshaw at Baguley Moor, Cheshire winning in twenty rounds. He followed that in 1843 with wins over Bill O'Brien in seventy two rounds, Jem Sheppard in eight rounds, at an unknown site near Manchester and finally a draw against Bob Martin in twenty six rounds at Dore Moor, near Sheffield, Yorkshire. The year of 1844 was just as successful for Massey with wins against Sam Brown at Cocks Bridge, near Manchester in a mammoth one hundred and two rounds and William Mills near Cudworth, near Barnsley, Yorkshire in seventy two rounds.

Now attracting gathering interest in the north he next faced the experienced and battle hardened Patsy Clay near Manchester in 1845 and in a tremendous struggle lasting seventy one rounds, Jem Massey was the eventual winner. His first opponent in 1846 was Bill Searle at Brierley Common, near Barnsley, with Massey winning in eighty four rounds and he followed this up by then trouncing the experienced and useful Enoch Horridge at Woodhead, Nottinghamshire in ten rounds. Young Reed, real name William Griffiths next entered the lists with Jem Massey at Hampton-in-Arden, near Birmingham and Massey was beaten, being disqualified in round sixty one when pulling his opponent to his feet after getting annoyed at Reed's continual dropping onto one knee.

Massey then took on the highly rated and unbeaten James Welsh, however when they met in 1847 at Long Reach, Cambridge it was Massey that won on a foul this time in round eighty nine of a titanic struggle. This win gained Massey general acclaim as the top man amongst the featherweights.

His next challenger was top rated Young Norley, three months later at Greenhithe, Kent and victory in sixty eight rounds gave Jem Massey the universal acclamation of being the best featherweight in the land. He only held on to this recognition for a for a little while though as he moved up in weight after the very clever and skilful Jem Edwards relieved him of that title when he beat Massey in fifty two rounds at Six Mile Bottom, Newmarket, Suffolk in 1848. Now struggling to make the featherweight class, Massey now moved up into the lightweights and in 1850 took on the unbeaten and capable Jerry Noon at Dean, Wiltshire, but was held to a draw when darkness beat them. A fifty six round win against James Welsh in 1851 at Long Reach, Cambridge catapulted Massey into the small band of top lightweights and he now touted himself as the lightweight king, although this was not universally accepted.

In 1852 Massey took on and beat highly rated Dan McNulty on a foul in sixty rounds at Long Reach, Cambridge and after fights in the same year and also 1853 against James Welsh failed to materialize it was not until 1854 that Massey entered the ring again. A second fight against McNulty was contested at Lower Hope, Tilbury, London, when again Massey was the victor in seventy six rounds. Increasing weight was now becoming a problem for Massey and by now being a publican as well did not help. When he met Bill Hayes at Bentley, Suffolk in 1856 the contest was made at 140lbs. in which they both huffed and puffed to a fifty one round draw after the first fight was disturbed by police after thirty six rounds but resumed at another venue.

This was Jem Massey's last fight and with his family they emigrated to New York and then to Canada, where he died in 1863.

1842

Jack Cronshaw, Baguley Moor, Cheshire	W	20r.	35min.	£10

1843

Bill O'Brien, Adgecroft Bridge, near Manchester	W	72r.	88min.	£10
Jem Sheppard, near Manchester	W	8r.	18min.	£20
Bob Martin, Dore Moor, near Sheffield, Yorks.	D	26r.		£8

185

1844

Sam Brown, Cocks Bridge, near Manchester	W	102r.	128min.	£50
William Mills, Cudworth, near Barnsley, Yorks.	W	72r.	80min.	£50

1845

Patsy Clay, near Manchester	W	71r.	76min.	£100

1846

Bill Searle, Cudworth, near Barnsley	W	84r.	150min.	£60
Enoch Horridge, Woodhead, Notts.	W	10r.	15min.	£200
Young Reed, Hampton-in-Arden, near Birmingham	LF	61r.	78min.	£100

1847

James Welsh, Long Reach, Cambridge	WF	88r.	135min.	£200

Now acclaimed as the best featherweight in the country.

Young Norley, Greenhithe, Kent	W	68r.	105min.	£200

1848

Jem Edwards, Six Mile Bottom, near Newmarket, Suffolk	L	52r.	194mins	£200

1850

Jerry Noon, Dean, Wilts.	D	88r.	178min.	£200

1851

James Welsh, Long Reach, Cambridge	WF	56r.	82min.	£200

1852

Dan McNulty, Long Reach, Cambridge	WF	60r.	113min.	£200

1854

Dan McNulty, Lower Hope, Tilbury, London	W	76r.	154min.	£200

1856

Bill Hayes, Bentley, Suffolk	D	51r.	112min.	£200

William Gill
(Acclaimed as the best in the land at featherweight 1848)

Born: 1820   Died: 1869

"Paddy"

Born in Dublin, but moving to Coventry with his parents when he was a boy Paddy Gill grew up to be a fine featherweight. Standing about 5' 6" high and weighing anywhere between 119-124lbs. his first recorded fight was as an 18 year old in 1838 against Bill Heap at Radford Common, Coventry and winning in fifty rounds, taking 75 minutes. Four years later he had a very profitable year winning all four fights; firstly against Charley Foster, then Tom Pritchard, followed by William Hubbard twice after their first bout was stopped by the police.

In 1843 he took on Ned Mosley at Tamworth, Staffordshire, winning in twelve rounds and then highly rated Young Norley, losing his first fight after going down in sixty nine rounds. In 1844 he picked up his winning ways again with the defeat of undefeated Jack Bethell somewhere near Birmingham in fifty eight rounds and then another win against the also unbeaten George Holden over twenty one rounds. The year 1845 found Gill facing Young Reed, a skilful but inexperienced fighter from London, at Ensham Common, near Oxford; however Reed gave Gill a tough grilling before being forced to give in after fifty nine rounds. Four months later Paddy Gill was entering the prize ring with Young Norley, who had given him his only defeat just over a couple of years earlier. They faced each other at Weedon, near Witney, Oxfordshire and in an historic fight noted for the sheer guts and bravery of Norley, Gill won in a bloody battle that lasted for just over 4 hours and a marathon one hundred and sixty rounds, in which Norley had to fight on the retreat from round eight, after he had fractured his collarbone when thrown by Gill.

Paddy Gill was now accepted as a premier featherweight and he carried on his winning ways the next year against Tommy Davis at Lindrick Common, Nottinghamshire, who unfortunately died of his injuries. In 1848 the veteran top featherweight Tom Maley the

"Bloomsbury Pet" was Gill's next opponent and another win was notched up over the veteran, although it took seventy seven rounds to subdue him, but Gill was now considered the best in the land. Paddy Gill was now coming to the end of his fighting career, first losing his title after being absent at the start of his fight with James Welsh in 1849 and having to forfeit the £100 purse and then in 1850 in a fight with Tom Griffiths at Frimley Green, Hampshire, Griffiths died after losing to Gill after fifty three rounds of fighting. Although Gill was acquitted of manslaughter he temporarily retired but in 1854 he attempted a comeback against Dan McNulty but lost in seventeen rounds.

1838
Bill Heap, Radford Common, Coventry	W	50r.	75min.	£10

1842
Charley Foster, Redgate, Atherton, Lancs.	W	57r.	135min.	£20
Tom Pritchard, unknown venue	W	12r.	30min.	£10
William Hubbard, near Bedworth, Warks. (stopped by police)	W	26r.	35min.	£50
William Hubbard, Caldecotte, Bucks.	W	42r.	70min.	£50

1843
Ned Mosley, Tamworth, Staffs.	W	12r.	25min.	£50
Young Norley, Northfleet, Kent	L	69r.	115min.	£100

1844
Jack Bethell, near Birmingham	W	58r.	82min.	£100
George Holden, Warwickshire	W	21r.	33min.	£100

1845
Young Reed, Ensham Common, Oxford	W	59r.	83min.	£20

1846
Young Norley, near Witney, Oxon.	W	160r.	247min.	£400

1847
Tommy Davis, Lindrick Common, Notts.	W	60r.	130min.	£120
Davies died from his injuries				

1848
Tom Maley, somewhere outside Andover	W	77r.	159r.	£200

1850
Tom Griffiths, Frimley Green, Hants	W	53r.	105min.	£200

1854
Dan McNulty, Long Reach, Whitstable, Kent	L	17r.	64min.	£200

Alf Walker
(Acclaimed as the best in the land at featherweight 1854-1859)

Born: 1826   Died: 1863

Alf Walker was the second and youngest of lightweight king Johnny Walker's brothers to follow him into the ring, although the other brother, Harry, retired after only two fights, losing on both occasions. Alf the youngest was a hard hitting pugilist, a bit on the crude side yet strong on stamina, standing 5' 6" and weighing 116lbs. He first fought and beat the heavier Tom Darby at Woking Common, Surrey in 1850 and then followed this up with a draw in his second fight, in 1852 with Jack Hicks at Long Reach, Kent, when darkness fell after three hours of fighting.

It was his third fight against the popularly accepted champion of the bantamweights, Joe Hoiles in April 1854 at Mildenhall, Suffolk that propelled Alf Walker to fame. After eight rounds Hoiles was comfortably in front when out of nowhere a thunderous right dropped Hoiles in round nine. Joe Hoiles was carried to the scratch by his seconds for the next round but it was no good, he was in no condition to continue and the recognition of champion of the bantamweights now passed to Walker. Although Joe Hoiles chased after Walker for a return, Alf Walker, like his brother Johnny, had a curious and successful knack of ducking challenges to his title, preferring to concentrate on his business affairs which included running the Duke of Argyle public house in London.

He carried on like this for several years, side stepping challenges to his title without actually announcing definite retirement, until in March 1859, with his various business ventures failing he agreed to a contest against the undefeated Bill Gilham from Brighton. Both men were evenly matched hard hitters but in round seven Gilham managed to throw Walker, who in turn landed heavily, dislocated his collarbone and was unable to continue. Although this fight did not gain the acclaim of being feted as the best featherweight in the land for Gilham, as he was considered over the weight limit, it did rule out Walker's pretensions to the claim from then on.

Walker's various business ventures went further downhill and in 1860 he abandoned his wife, his family and the public house emigrating to America where rumour has it he joined the Union forces in the American Civil War and was believed to have been killed at the Battle of Gettysburg in July 1863. This has never been proved but Alf Walker was never heard of again.

1850
Thomas Darby, Woking Common, Surrey   W   48r.   83min.   £20

1852
Jack Hicks, Long Reach, Kent   D   95r.   165min.   £50

1854
Joe Hoiles, Mildenhall, Suffolk   W   9r.   17min.   £200
Now acclaimed as the best featherweight in the country.

1859
Bill Gilham, London area   L   7r.   20min.   £100

Joe Nolan
(Acclaimed as the best in the land at featherweight 1857-1858)

Born: 1839   Died: 1867

Joe Nolan from Birmingham was born in September 1839 and was described by many experts at the time as being one of the hottest prospects from the Midlands for many years. Apparently a pleasant and easy going sort of fellow outside the ring, he was a clever boxer with quick hands and feet inside it. Standing 5' 5½" tall and weighing around 122lbs. when in perfect condition and he seemed to have the fistic world at his feet. However, his one big flaw was the fatal combination of a complete hatred of any form of training and an ever increasing love of gin.

His first recorded fight for a purse was against Jack Robinson in December 1855, at an unknown destination in the Midlands. After forty rounds, lasting 55 minutes had been fought, the police intervened and the contest was declared a draw. In March 1857 Nolan came up against Jack Flanery, held just outside Birmingham, which Nolan won in a titanic battle of ninety five rounds, lasting just over two hours. Nolan now claimed to be the top featherweight in the country, a term that had been introduced a few years earlier to recognize fighters up to about 126lbs. Putting on weight naturally coupled with unhealthy living, Nolan moved up to take on the lightweights and after beating Bill Ensor, a Birmingham man, in fifty two rounds at Stratford-on-Avon, Warwickshire in April 1858, he next took on George Henley in August of the same year, winning in thirty rounds; Joe Nolan now claimed himself to be the king of the lightweights as well, although this was not recognized outside his own ego.

Because of his abundance of natural ability he was able to wing it in the prize ring at the beginning of his career, although constantly going missing from his training camps had its effect on his form. Even when not fully fit he was still too good for fighters such as the battle hardened Jack Hicks, who was beaten twice in succession, in March 1859 at Aldershot, Hampshire, Nolan winning in forty eight rounds and then again in February 1860 in sixty six rounds.

During his training for the impending fight with Dan Thomas, Nolan's backers sent a pair of strict trainers to look after him; however they were unable to curb his escapades with the gin bottle. On one occasion they eventually found him in a tavern in such a drunken stupor that he could only be roused when doused in buckets of cold water. These two trainers were dismissed and a new man, Joe Wareham was hired. Joe Wareham turned out to be even craftier than Joe Nolan and made sure his disappearances were halted by handcuffing himself to the fighter at night! The daytime hours were spent in exercises while wrapped in sweaters and blankets, to sweat off the excess poundage Nolan had gained, in a rush to get him somewhere near peak fitness in time for the forthcoming fight with Thomas, albeit at the expense of weakening Nolan through this method. This desperate method was forced on Wareham as Nolan's backers had signed articles for Nolan to fight Thomas at 122lbs. for the chance to be accepted as the premier featherweight in the country.

Dan Thomas, a rugged Welshman was known for his terrific stamina and considerable experience gained in the tough environment of mixing with the tough Welsh mountain fighters. The venue was to be Wallingford in Berkshire, but because of police interference before the start of the fight everyone changed trains at Reading and on to Aldermaston, Berkshire where a ring was set up but the fight was interrupted again by the law. It continued further down the line at Kintbury, Berkshire but in an uneventful and dreary fight it was finally declared a draw. Joe Nolan only fought once more; in 1864 he took on Dick Fellowes at Four Ashes, Staffordshire, however after twenty rounds once again the police intervened and so the fight was declared a draw.

Because of his drinking and wild living Joe Nolan was dead before his 28th birthday in 1867.

1855

Jack Robinson, Midlands District	D	40r.	55min.	£30
(stopped by police)				

1857

Jack Flanery, Rubery Hill, nr. Birmingham	W	95r.	130min.	£20

Now acclaimed as the best featherweight in the country.

1858

Bill Ensor, Stratford-on-Avon, Warks.	W	52r.	70min.	£20
George Henley, unknown venue	W	30r.	32min.	£50

1859
| Jack Hicks, nr. Aldershot, Hampshire | W | 48r. | 85min. | £120 |

1860
| Jack Hicks, unknown venue | W | 66r. | 165min. | £240 |

1862
| Dan Thomas, Aldermaston/Kintbury, Berks. | D | 20r. | 90min. | £400 |

1864
| Dick Fellowes, Four Ashes, Staffs.
(stopped by police) | D | 20r. | 85min. | £5 |

Bill Gilham
(Acclaimed as the best in the land at featherweight 1858-1860)

Born: 1834   Died: 1891

Bill Gilham was born in Brighton in March 1834, however nothing is known about his early life in the Sussex seaside town. As a prize fighter he stood 5' 4½" tall and weighed around 118lbs. and was known as a hard hitting, durable fighter. Gilham opened his prize fighting account against Joe Coombs at Hayling Island, Hampshire in June 1852, eventually beating Coombs after one hundred and four rounds. Exactly a year later and again at Hayling Island he drew with Teddy Mottle when they fought to a standstill after one hundred and twenty rounds, lasting 165 minutes and all for a purse of just twenty pounds! His next fight in July 1858 was against Scuttle Rogers at an unknown venue and Rogers was taken out in a much shorter fight of thirty four rounds, lasting 45 minutes and once again for a purse of twenty pounds. Twice, at the end of that year Gilham took on highly rated Alec Andrews, the first encounter in November ending in a draw after thirty four rounds, the second fight, a month later at Ash Common, Surrey, resulting in a win for Gilham in the same number of rounds as the first fight.

Gilham claimed the featherweight championship but this was not generally recognized as Alf Walker was the generally accepted champion although inactive at the time. In 1859 the two met, although Gilham was over the generally accepted featherweight limit, and beating Walker in just seven rounds, lasting just 20 minutes. Walker was unfortunate as he had to give in with a dislocated shoulder after being thrown by Gilham.

Gilham immediately realized he could not keep getting down to the accepted weight limit to keep participating for this title, so he casually claimed the lightweight crown instead, stating that he would be prepared to defend it against anyone. No one really took any notice of Gilham's claim, which showed in the February of the next year, when he was only second billing to the Joe Nolan v. Jack Hicks fight, in a quickly organized set-to against Jerry Hawkes. In the contest itself against Hawkes, held on the banks of the River Thames, Gilham won in thirteen rounds, but his purse money was again only twenty pounds, not exactly a so-called champion's bounty! Whatever claim Bill Gilham had on any accolade was dashed in May 1860, when he came up against Dan Thomas and in a tough, bruising battle which he lost after 165 minutes, taking up forty eight rounds, with Thomas now more legitimately claiming the top position. Gilham then drew with Tom Tyler but the police intervened after thirty two rounds at Smugoak Common, Hertfordshire later that year.

For the next six years there are no records of fights for Gilham, although it is known that he got married in 1861, had two sons and was living in his home town of Brighton. Presumably still living in Brighton in 1866 he fought Jack Brookes in Sussex in April of that year, resulting in another draw, this time in twenty rounds, lasting just over an hour. Whether police intervened or injury to one of the fighters bought this fight to an end is not reported.

Bill Gilham was next involved in a turn up with Tim Collins on a hot day in July 1868 after the Reading Races at Kings Meadows. Apparently getting involved in an argument with the London based pugilist Collins, they decided to settle their differences in the shade of the trees, the fight ending in a foul by Gilham in round fifteen, but the result proved unsatisfactory to all and so they fought a second fight there and then which ended in round ten, when Gilham had to retire through injury. He swore he would get his revenge on Collins but there is no record of Gilham ever fighting again and Collins emigrated to the United States shortly afterwards anyway, where he won short lived fame and notoriety.

Gilham then retired and became a fishmonger, rising to master fishmonger, ending up living in London with his second wife.

1852

Joe Coombes, Hayling Island, Hants.	W	104r.	113min.

1855

Teddy Mottle, Hayling Island, Hants.	D	122r.	165min. £20

1858

Scuttle Rogers, unknown venue	W	34r.	45min. £20
Alec Andrews, unknown venue	D	34r.	37min. £50
Alec Andrews, Ash Common, Surrey	W	34r.	56min. £50
Now acclaimed as the best featherweight in the country.			
Alf Walker, London area	W	7r.	20min. £100
Now acclaimed as the best lightweight in the country.			

1860

Jerry Hawkes, beside River Thames (turn up)	W	13r.	25min.	£20
Dan Thomas, London area	L	48r.	165min.	£200
Tom Tyler, Smugoak Common, Herts. (stopped by police)	D	32r.	100min.	£100

1866

Jack Brookes, Sussex	D	22r.	66min.	£50

1868

Tim Collins, King's Meadows, Reading	L	15r.	25min.	
Tim Collins, King's Meadows, Reading	L	10r.	25min.	£10+purse

Dan Thomas

(Acclaimed as the best in the land at featherweight 1860-1862)

Born: 1828   Died: 1910

"Dan Pontypridd"

Dan Thomas never fought outside his native Wales until he was in his thirties, only then setting off for London to try his luck in the capital. Born in Pontypridd in 1828 he stood about 5' 4" tall and weighed about 116lbs. He was so proud of his birthplace that he began calling himself Dan Pontypridd. He was a rugged, mauling type of fighter with tremendous stamina, always training hard for his fights. Coupled with a large dose of caution he was able to gradually and relentlessly wear down his opponents instead of trying to take them out quickly. He was reputed to have been discovered and backed by Johnny Walker the old lightweight champion when Walker spotted him on a visit to South Wales.

Thomas took part in many unrecorded fights over the years around his local stamping grounds in South Wales against local fighters, some of them probably being some of the formidable mountain fighters. His first recorded bout was against Jemmy Williams at Machen, Caerphilly, South Wales in July 1855, winning in fifty tremendous rounds. He lost his next fight in February 1856 against David "Duck" Ingrams, being beaten in thirty five rounds, somewhere in Monmouthshire. He got back to winning ways in his English debut when beating Jack Brookes at Dagenham, London in October 1858, winning in fifty five rounds and he immediately claimed to be the bantamweight title holder. He then beat the clever colourful American Charlie Lynch in January 1859 at Aldershot Common, winning in fifty six rounds lasting over 90 minutes in a catch weight contest, as by this time Thomas was over the estimated weight limit.

In May 1860 he came up against the well-respected Bill Gillam and Thomas was eventually the winner in a tremendous contest in which it took him nearly three hours and 48 rounds to subdue Gillam at a venue somewhere in the London area. With this momentous win Dan

Thomas now made a claim for the featherweight title and later in the year was presented with a commemorative belt supporting his claim, from his friends and supporters.

On hearing this claim, Joe Nolan's backers challenged Dan Thomas to put his money where his mouth was and meet their man, the winner to be recognized as the undisputed featherweight champion. Thomas was more than happy to defend his claim as he did not hold the fleet footed Nolan in very high esteem anyway, knowing that Nolan's fitness was always suspect due to a hatred of serious training. The backers of Thomas pressed for a purse of £500 a side with the weight limit to be set at 120lb. Nolan's side countered with a purse of £200 and the weight limit to be 122lbs. Thomas refused these terms at first, until it was pointed out to him that it was for the title and that Nolan's camp could not find that amount of purse money plus he could also risk losing the chance to take on Nolan for the unquestionable right to be called champion. General opinion backed Nolan's side, so finally Thomas relented and the contracts were drawn up. The venue was originally somewhere around Wallingford in Berkshire, but because of police interference even before the start of the fight everyone dispersed and caught the train back to Reading where they changed trains and carried on to Aldermaston, Berkshire where a ring was set up, but the fight was again interrupted by the law. Again they set off further down the line to Kintbury, Berkshire where the ring was set up. The fight itself was an uneventful fight as the cat and mouse tactics of Thomas against a relatively unfit Nolan, so cancelling each other out. In fact the referee asked both fighters from time to time for more action, which eventually roused Thomas into start throwing some meaningful punches, but the fight was finally declared a draw after twenty rounds over 1½ hours of still relatively sparse activity.

This was Dan Thomas's last fight in the prize ring, but the durable Welshman lived to a ripe age of 82, dying in his beloved Pontypridd as a celebrated pugilist.

1855

Jemmy Williams, Machen, South Glamorgan	W	50r.	71min.	£40

1856

David Ingram, Monmouthshire	L	35r.	50min.	£50

1858

Jack Brookes, Dagenham, London	W	55r.	97min.	£50

Now acclaimed to be the best bantamweight in the land.

1859
Charley Lynch, Aldershot Common, Hants.   W   56r.   100min.   £100

1860
Bill Gilham, London area   W   48r.   165min.   £200
Now acclaimed to be the best featherweight in the land.

1862
Joe Nolan, Aldermaston/Kintbury, Berks.   D   20r.   90min.   £400
(The referee stopped the bout and it was alleged Thomas received £25 to take the draw).

Alec Lawson was considered by some as a featherweight champion after Dan Thomas retired however it was only the first half of his rather sketchy ring career that his contests were fought with bare knuckles and from 1872 he fought with gloves.

THE BANTAMWEIGHTS

Bantamweight was a weight class that probably evolved in the 1850's and derived the name from the fighting bantam cocks that took part in the illegal, but popular sport of cock fighting. It was certainly established before the advent of the Queensbury Rules in 1868. The weight class was established for the men who weighed less than 116lb. approximately, although as already stated as with the other weight classifications in this book these weight limits are only rough guides.

Joe Hoiles
(Acclaimed as the best in the land at bantamweight 1851-1854)

Born: 1829   Died: 1860

"The Spider"

Born in Bethnall Green, London, Joe Hoiles stood 5' 6" and his heaviest fighting weight was only 96lbs.-110lbs. Because he found difficulty in finding challengers at this weight most fights were against heavier men. He made his début in 1848 when he beat Jem Cornwell at Woking, Surrey in just over 30 minutes, but it wasn't until 1850 that he fought again finding it hard to secure opponents at his own weight of around 98lbs. In that year and now weighing around 102lbs. he fought the then undefeated Jem "The Mouse" Herbert, again at Woking, Surrey and in an evenly fought contest it took Hoiles one hundred rounds to finally subdue Herbert. Building himself up to 105lbs. he next beat Jemmy Madden convincingly at Edenbridge, Kent claiming the bantamweight title at the same time. He was then lucky to receive a draw against Harry Adams at Lower Hope Point, Kent in 1851, after the referee judged that they were both using foul blows and maybe got the decision because he was the lesser culprit!

In September 1851 Jem Trainer was Joe Hoiles next opponent and after an even first few rounds Hoiles eventually stopped his man in round forty nine and was now generally accepted as the best in his class and therefore the champion, although the title was still unofficial. In April 1853 he met Bill Bowers from Billingsgate and after a dispute at first about weight, as Hoiles only weighed 105lbs. compared to Bowers at 114lbs. the fight eventually got under way with Hoiles fighting at long distance in the opening rounds. After an hour with Bowers now well beaten, Hoiles hurled his man to the ground and with that Bowers seconds threw in the sponge to save their man further punishment. This left Joe Hoiles undisputed champion and recognized by the Fancy and the sporting press as king of the bantamweights.

Thoughts of retirement on Hoiles part, through lack of suitable opponents, were changed when accepting the challenge of Alf

Walker, younger brother of former lightweight kingpin, Johnny Walker. Walker was one of those fighters who bordered on the then recognized bantam/featherweight limit and so by losing a little weight could also fight at bantamweight. They met at Mildenhall, Suffolk in April 1854 and up until round eight Hoiles was considered to be ahead, but a terrific right hand by Walker in round nine caught Hoiles unawares and he was knocked out cold and with it went his title. Although Walker promised Joe Hoiles a return match, he instead immediatel vacated the bantamweight class and Hoiles rejected a challenge from Jack Hicks on the grounds of Hicks weight 116lbs. being too much weight to give away. Walker continued to sidestep any challenges to his title and so Hoiles assumed the title of champion again although no-one took much notice; in the meantime the featherweight limit was unofficially set at up to 126lbs. with Walker claiming this accolade as he now fell into that category, a weight that he was better recognized at but then ducked challenges to this claim.

Alf Walker never did give Joe Hoiles a rematch and so Joe Hoiles retired, only to return in exhibition bouts when his pub venture failed and after a long illness he died at the age of 31 years old.

1848

Jack Cornwell, Woking Common, Surrey	W	18r.	29min.	£20

1850

Jemmy Herbert, Woking Common, Surrey	W	100r.	135min.	£50
Jemmy Madden, Edenbridge, Kent	W	56r.	91min.	£30

1851

Harry Adams, Lower Hope Point, Kent	D	97r.	120min.	£50
James Trainer, Long Reach, Kent	W	49r.	80min.	£100

Now acclaimed as the best bantamweight in the country.

1853

Bill Bowers, Long Reach, Kent	W	25r.	84min.	£100

1854

Alf Walker, Mildenhall, Suffolk	L	9r.	17min.	£200

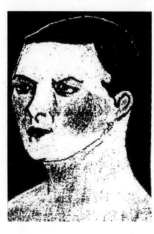

Charlie Lynch
(Acclaimed as the best in the land at bantamweight 1859-1861)

Born: 1836   Died: 1866

Charlie Lynch, an American by birth fled from his native country after the death of one Andy Kelly in a fight in September 1856 and arrived in London a month later, but it wasn't until October 1857 that he found an opponent. That was Simon Finighty, a scientific boxer compared with Lynch who at only 5' 3" and weighing 112lbs. was a tough, durable slugger and it was no surprise when Finighty built up a considerable lead with his superior punching and ring work, however Lynch was still hanging on in there three hours later. With darkness falling and Lynch almost blinded he swung wildly while Finighty was on his knees and was disqualified.

Lynch was next up against John "Young" Harrington, a former contender and when they met in June 1858 at Canvey Island, Essex, Lynch pummelled Harrington to defeat. Jack Sullivan, his next opponent went the same way as John Harrington and with no more 112lb. men willing to meet him Lynch agreed to take on 120lb. Welshman Dan Thomas in January 1859 on Aldershot Common, Hampshire and another tough slugger who out-slugged Charlie Lynch and forced Lynch to submit in round fifty six. After this defeat a rematch with Simon Finighty was made for August 1859 at Kent Marshes and in an even fight in which Finighty landed more, but lighter blows it was Lynch's heavier punches especially to the body that won the day forcing Finighty to retire after round forty two. Up to that point Finighty was recognized as the best 112lb. fighter in the land, Lynch now assumed the mantle as the best and as a result of a subscription, a belt was presented to him at a benefit in his honour.

Charlie Lynch then challenged all comers again at 112lbs. for the title and next fought the novice Bill Shaw in April 1860 at Purfleet, Kent. In a hard fought contest and with Lynch apparently the worse off, the police intervened after about an hour and so the fight was resumed the next day at Walton on Thames, Surrey where the two fighters continued for another sixty one rounds before Charlie Lynch had to bow to the superiority of Bill Shaw. Although Bill Shaw found himself king of the bantamweights he never defended the title, as he immediately moved up in weight. Lynch therefore retained his claim and then defended it against another novice, George Holden in December 1861 and when after fifty three rounds of brutal fighting, Holden, through closing, swollen eyes managed to throw Lynch, rendering him unconscious. George Holden now found himself in the exalted position of being recognized as the best bantamweight around.

1856

Andy Kelly, Hyers Landing, USA	W	86r.		

1857

Tough Gilbert, *unknown venue*	W			£8
Simon Finighty, Old Haven, London	LF	95r.	168min.	£30

1858

Young Harrington, Shell Haven, Kent	W	58r.	77min.	£50
Jack Sullivan, London area	W	29r.	48min.	£55

1859

Dan Thomas, Aldershot Common, Hants.	L	56r.	100min.	£100
Simon Finighty, Kent Marshes	WF	43r.	70min.	£100

Now acclaimed as the best bantamweight in the country.

1860

Bill Shaw, Purfleet, Essex (stopped by police)	D	37r.	60min.	
Bill Shaw, Walton-on-Thames, Middx.	L	61r.	45min.	£50

1861

George Holden, London area	L	54r.	84min.	£50

George Holden
(Acclaimed as the best in the land at bantamweight 1861-1862)

Born: 1842   Died: 1916

George Holden was the son of another well known bare knuckle prize fighter also named George Holden who had fought around the Birmingham area in the mid 1840's and who had come up against and lost to the outstanding fighter Paddy Gill.

Young George Holden, who only stood 5' 3½" and weighing 112lbs. travelled to London putting up at Alec Keene's headquarters in the Three Tuns public and sporting house. Holden was a well-built pugilist and because it was his first recorded fight, albeit against the self-acclaimed bantamweight champion, Charlie Lynch, little notice of the contest was taken by the public and it was only a small crowd that attended the fight in December 1861 somewhere in the London area. Those who didn't attend missed a hard and evenly fought fight until round fifty four when suddenly Holden found the correct leverage to throw Charlie Lynch to the ground with such force that Lynch was knocked out cold and with it passed his title claim to young George Holden in his first recorded professional fight.

The next year, in August 1862 Holden was, in his second fight, after disposing of one title claimant in his first fight, meeting a man who was already regarded by many to be the best bantamweight in the land, Peter Morris. For this fight Holden was in top condition, training yet again in Alec Keene's pub while Morris trained at the Blue Anchor pub in Shoreditch, London, but apparently, due to sickness the training of Morris was interrupted and he was probably not in the best of condition when he entered the ring. The beginning of the fight it was pretty evens but by round twenty six, when the law intervened, Holden was having the worst of it and although he carried on until round sixty four, after the ring had been set up elsewhere, his father, who was his second, threw in the sponge thus ending George Holden's brief claim to fame.

In 1863 Holden fought and lost to Jack Lead, a leading contender at Kentish Marshes, in forty two rounds, but then won against a relatively unknown Mick Moran in twenty rounds in 1864 at

Cannock, Staffordshire. He did get a second shot at Peter Morris four years later, which is related in the ring career of Peter Morris.

1861

Charley Lynch, London area	W	54r.	84min.	£50

Now acclaimed as the best bantamweight in the country.

1862

Peter Morris, London area	L	64r.	129min.	£200

1863

Jack Lead, Kentish Marshes	L	42r.	73min.	£100

1864

Mick Moran, near Cannock, Staffs.	W	20r.	41min.	£30

1866

Peter Morris, Eckington, Derbys.	D	8r.		£200
Peter Morris, Croxwell Pk, Derbys.	D	34r.	112min.	

Peter Morris
(Acclaimed as the best in the land at bantamweight 1862-1870)

Born: 1840   Died: 1873

"The Mouse"

Born in Birmingham Peter Morris first fought at 15 years old losing to another novice and it was three years before entered the prize ring again. In 1858 near Birmingham he beat Jack Bayliss and Jack Dymock twice. His winning ways carried on in 1859 against Tom Rafferty at Cannock Chase, Staffordshire and then in 1861 he also defeated the best that London could throw at him including Jack Hartley, the highly rated Jem Fox and then George Holden, the title claimant, who was defeated by Morris in August 1862, so recognizing Morris as the new bantamweight supreme. Standing only 5' 3" and weighing just 100lbs. Morris met the older, heavier and experienced Maurice Roberts at catch weight in September 1863 and finished him off in round forty one. Morris then challenged the world at his own weight of just over 105lbs. but as there were no takers at that weight Morris found himself virtually retired for the next couple of years.

By 1866 two of the most prominent fighters were still Jem Fox and George Holden and it was Jem Fox at just under 112lb. that next met Peter Morris in April 1866 at Burton-on-Trent, Staffordshire, Morris being the winner after just over an hour of boxing. Again the gauntlet was thrown down by Morris willing to meet any man at 105lb.-112lb. which was immediately taken up by the fighter he had beaten four years earlier, George Holden and the fight was scheduled for November 1866 at Ekington, Derbyshire. In round seven the law intervened so the fight was continued the next day at Croxwell Park, Derbyshire, where Morris, showing his superb boxing ability, gradually brought Holden to his knees, however Holden's great durability enabled him a brief respite when he managed to close the left eye of Morris, but by round forty one Morris was back in charge, when again the law intervened in the proceedings. On the next day Kingswood Common in Shropshire was chosen, however mobs from the Birmingham area spoilt the arrangements and the continuation of the fight was suspended until further notice. Both boxers were taken to court for participating in the fight but released on bail but for George Holden it was his last fight as he retired to carry on being the full time landlord of the pub he had been running for some time.

Peter Morris did not fight again until he was scheduled to meet Harry Taylor in September 1868 at Four Ashes in Staffordshire but was again thwarted by the law who arrived as the ring was being erected. He was chased for a couple of miles by the police and was later, when caught, bound over to keep the peace.

His last fight was against Frank Wilson who he met at Birmingham in February 1870, where in the eighth round Wilson is supposed to have bitten Morris and Wilson's backer called on his man to quit as he thought he would not get a fair decision from the referee. This decision did cost Wilson the fight without deciding who would eventually have been the winner.

1858

Jack Bayliss, Rubery Hill, Birmingham	W	38r.	50min.	£20
Jack Dymock, Kings Norton, Leics.	D	7r.		£20
Jack Dymock, Lichfield, Staffs.	W	26r.	51min.	£30

1859

Tom Rafferty, Cannock Chase, Staffs.	W	16r.	22min.	£20

1860

Jack Hartley, London area	W	94r.	243min.	£50

1861

Jem Fox, Hednesford, Staffs.	W	36r.	50min.	£40

1862

Jack Hartley, London area	W	59r.	137min.	£50
George Holden, London area	W	64r.	129min.	£200

Now acclaimed as the best bantamweight in the country.

1863

Morris Roberts, London area	WF	41r.	138min.	£200

1866

Jem Fox, Burton-on-Trent, Derbys.	W	35r.	64min.	£100
George Holden, Eckington, Derbys. (stopped by police)	D	8r.		£200
George Holden, Croxwell Pk, Derbys. (stopped by police)	D	34r.	112min.	
George Holden, Kingswood Common, Derbys.	NC (stakes withdrawn)			

1870

Frank Wilson, Birmingham   WF   8r   30min.   £15 purse

With the formation of the Pelican Club followed by the National Sporting Club a few years later the weight classes were fixed within certain limits plus more definitive weight classes. Bare knuckle fighters who followed Morris as acclaimed bantamweight champions although they never had very distinguished ring careers were George Cunningham, Wolf Cohen and George Dove. Dove started his ring career as a bare knuckler but most of his contests were with gloves.

End of an Era

Although this book only describes many of the prominent bare knuckle pugilists up until 1870, some carried on with this illegal form of fighting for a few more years. Many of the more successful bare knuckle fighters emigrated to America where it was still widely practiced and some to Australia, New Zealand and South Africa.

As the Queensbury Rules of 1867 advised the use of gloves and set timed rounds and coupled with better training methods, many fighters discovered they suffered less physical damage to their bodies and fists, which meant they could engage in more fights and therefore earn more money. The sport became more organized and was eventually supervised by a legal controlling authority, The National Sporting Club. Some men's ring records show a mixture of gloved fights alongside some bareknuckle fights and this is why I have ended the book in 1870 as from around about this time this practice became more prevalent and I decided to keep the book to recorded bare knuckle contests only.

It can be safely said though that bare knuckle prize fights had almost died out by the 1890's, although like today there are still small pockets of participation taking place, especially amongst the travelling community.

The Fancy

There is mention throughout this book of the Fancy which was a word used to describe the particular followers of any sport of those days such as horse racing, cock fighting, dog fighting etc., and boxing was no exception. Interest in prize fighting ranged across the whole spectrum of English society from the very poor and criminally motivated to the very top, including some members of royalty. Many top class fights found commoners and nobility rubbing shoulders around the ringside, in their shared interest, because many of these fights attracted thousands of people to the countryside on the edge of London or other cities, or the commons, meadows and fields of rural England.

Before 1750 prize fighting was mostly consigned to the boxing academies such as those of James Figg and Jack Broughton's in London and one or two others in the capital. For these fights or demonstrations of boxing skills by well-known boxers of the day, posters were displayed; tickets were sold to the public which resulted in a large number of the nobility and the famous attending these events. After the backer of Broughton, the Duke of Cumberland lost a heavy wager on his man when he was beaten by Jack Slack in 1750 and then lost another large sum of money on Slack when he was beaten; he closed down his academy and had boxing made illegal.

With the sport forced out of the capital the venues and arrangements had to be secretly arranged, to stop magistrates outlawing the fights and the law breaking up contests, with the majority of the supporters being notified at the last possible moment. Sadly, the criminal element always seemed to know as well and followed the coaches, carts and pedestrians out of town. Many of the criminal element were attracted to the fights, not for the sport, but for the rich pickings which could be made from the wealthy men-about-town attending at ringside. Pickpockets, cardsharps, thieves and prostitutes mingled amongst the crowds looking for victims amongst the more privileged of Regency and later Victorian society. Landlords of inns and hostelries surrounding a fight venue also profited from a prize fight in their area along with the extra income from lodgings, eating and drinking before and after a fight.

In all, for a lot of people who attended these occasions it was a day out, especially for the poor who led mostly miserable, wretched lives, it was a memorable event, something to celebrate and look back upon and to say, I was there. Many of the fights, especially those arranged on the same day as a horse race meeting such as at Ascot, usually took place after the last race of a day that was packed with music, fairs and sideshows.

Even when they were not fighting, many of the well-known pugilists either held classes or lessons for mostly the idle rich, who would pay good money for lessons in self-defence, or they would tour the country taking part in exhibitions at county and country fairs to earn extra money.

Purse Money

Purse money was usually put up by the well-to-do patrons who backed a fighter they believed could make them even more money by betting on their fights as well. As many ex-pugilists owned or ran public houses, these haunts were used by the boxing fraternity; a deposit for a forthcoming contest was often lodged there by the backers or with the landlord. The rest of the money was then arranged to be paid by a certain date named in the articles drawn up for the contest, either in instalments or in full. The combatants would normally have a bet on themselves (a side stake) usually laid just before the fight and the winner would normally collect all the purse and side stake money, unless a certain amount was arranged to be paid to the loser in the articles. Another way the loser might receive a few pounds would be if a collection was made at ringside or the winner gave him a small amount for putting up a brave show. Many smaller fights would rely on coins thrown in the ring after the fight and shared accordingly. Many boxers would also receive extra money or a bonus from their backer(s) for winning, especially if the backers had won large wagers themselves on their fighter.

Although many purses seem relatively small in today's money for the pain and exertions the fighters went through to win it, the table below gives an approximate indication of what some purses were worth when compared to today's figures (2011).

2011		1750	1820	1850	1870
Purse money					
£10	=	£847	£419	£585	£457
£50	=	£4,237	£2,096	£2,926	£2,285
£100	=	£8,475	£4,192	£5,853	£4,570
£200	=	£16,950	£8,384	£11,706	£9,140
£400	=	£33,900	£16,768	£23,412	£18,280

Trophies and Belts

With the birth of prize fighting in the early 18th century the fighters fought for fame and money, with the earliest recorded mention of something apart from money being a medal presented to Daniel Mendoza, Champion of England 1792-1795. It was not until the early 19th century that the rich backers and patrons of the most prominent pugilists started to present them with trophies, belts, medals etc., along with their prize money.

The first known trophy in 1811, bought by subscription, by gentlemen of the Fancy, was awarded to Tom Cribb, Champion of England 1808-1822, rewarding his two epic fights against the black American Tom Molineaux. The trophy was presented to Cribb at a dinner in Bob Gregson's Chop House in London to acknowledge his beating off the American challenge. These dinners attended by the rich patrons of the Fancy and well known bruisers of the day, became a common practice in the first thirty years or so of the 19th century, celebrating and rewarding past and present noted boxers.

When Cribb retired he was also awarded a lion-skin belt and he handed his title to Tom Spring, but not the trophy, which he decided to keep. From the 1820's the presenting of a trophy or cup, but mostly a belt became popular as an accolade to that particular fighter's prowess in the prize ring and which they retained after they retired. The earliest recorded belt that was transferred from one champion to another seems to be when in 1839, after Bendigo had beaten Deaf Burke to claim the title; he received a belt awarded to Jem Ward for his 1825 championship win against Tom Cannon. Bendigo however refused to forfeit the belt claiming it was a gift! In 1855 a new championship belt was introduced which did pass down from champion to champion, starting with Tom Sayers in 1857 through to Jem Mace, who, after defeating Joe Goss twice, in 1863 and 1866 decided that it was his by right. Mace seemed to have a perchance for collecting trophies, cups, silver plates, medals and belts awarded to him by various sources and so he decided he would also add this belt to his collection as well!

With the 1867 publication of the Queensbury Rules recommending the wearing of gloves and timed rounds amongst other changes, bare knuckle prize fighting was in rapid decline. The Marquis of

215

Queensbury now presented silver cups for Heavyweight, Middleweight and Lightweight in a competition where gloves were always worn, to the recently formed Amateur Boxing Club in London. This tradition carried on until 1885 when it became the Amateur Boxing Association. From 1909 a belt known as the Lonsdale Belt was presented to championship winners of all weights under the Queensbury Rules by the National Sporting Club, founded on 1891 and is unchanged until this day.

Glossary of Terms

Many terms were used in the eloquent description of fight reports in Regency and Victorian newspapers and books. So as not to confuse the reader I have avoided using them in most cases. However below are some of the more common words used to describe a bare knuckle fight in those days including some of the sayings that we use today which derived from the sport.

Bottom – Showing plenty of courage and bravery.

Colours – A ribbon, handkerchief or small piece of cloth in the preferred colours of the fighter that was usually tied to the ring post in the corner that he presided during a fight. The winner usually collected the losers colours at the end of the fight.

Cross – A fixed fight.

Cross buttock throw – Ability to throw an opponent over your hips to the ground therefore ending the round.

Fib – Short or half arm punch.

Leveller – A punch that knocks your opponent to the ground.

Milling – General feinting, footwork and light punches to test opponent.

Mufflers – Gloves or mitts used in training, sparring or exhibition bouts.

Raw 'uns – Bare fists.

Spilling the claret – Bleeding due to cuts to the body and face etc.

Suit in chancery – Trapping an opponent's head under your arm while continuously hitting him with your other fist.

Turn-up – An unscheduled fight or street brawl.

To come up to scratch or to toe the line – A line or small square was scratched into the ground inside the ring which the fighters had to come up to at the start of each round, if they failed then they conceded the fight.

To throw in the towel – When a fighter could not continue his seconds threw a towel or sponge into the ring to signal that they were withdrawing their fighter.

To throw your hat into the ring – Before a fight commenced the fighters threw their hats into the ring to show their intention to fight or to meet the challenge of their opponent.